THE NEXT POPE

GEORGE WEIGEL

THE NEXT POPE

*The Office of Peter and
a Church in Mission*

IGNATIUS PRESS　　SAN FRANCISCO

Cover Art:
Saint Peter in Cathedra
Bronze sculpture
Arnolfo di Cambio (1245–1302)
St. Peter's Basilica, Vatican State
© Photograph by Stefano Spaziani

Cover design by Enrique J. Aguilar

CONTENTS

A BRIEF EXPLANATORY NOTE

Over the past three decades, I have had the privilege of extended conversations with Pope John Paul II, Pope Emeritus Benedict XVI, and Pope Francis. What I learned from those encounters—and from many years of interaction with Catholics on every continent, living all stations of life in the Church—has prompted the reflections in this book.

What follows, therefore, is a partial payment on a large debt.

The Catholic Church is the same Church over time, for as Saint Paul reminds us in Ephesians 4:5, it serves the same Lord, is formed by the same faith, and is born from the same baptism. The Catholic mode of being-the-Church changes, however, to meet the demands of continuing Christ's saving mission in the world. There have been five such epochal transitions in Christian history. One of them is underway now.

In the first of these great transitions, what we know as the Early Church definitively separated from what became rabbinic Judaism, in a process that accelerated after the First Jewish-Roman War in 70 A.D. That Early Church gave way to, even as it gave birth to, Patristic Christianity, which emerged in the fourth century and was shaped by the Church's encounter with classical culture. Toward the end of the first millennium, Patristic Christianity gave way to, even as it gave birth to, Medieval Christendom, the closest synthesis of Church, culture, and society ever achieved. Medieval Christendom fractured in the several Reformations of the sixteenth century, and from that cataclysm came Counter-Reformation Catholicism: the mode of being the Church in which every Catholic born before the mid-1950s grew up.

And toward the end of the second millennium, the fifth great transition began to gather force throughout the world Church: from Counter-Reformation Catholicism to the Church of the New Evangelization. Catholics live today within the turbulence of this transitional moment.

In the third decade of the twenty-first century, the Catholic Church finds itself at a critical breakpoint in that fifth epochal transition. For the three popes I have personally known and whose Petrine ministries I have closely followed have all, in one way or another, been men of the Second Vatican Council: the event that fully set in motion the transition from Counter-Reformation Catholicism to the Church of the New Evangelization. The next pope, though, will not have been shaped by Vatican II in the same way as his three predecessors in the Chair of Saint Peter.

As a very junior Polish bishop and later the archbishop of Kraków, Karol Wojtyła (the future Pope John Paul II) took an active role in all four periods of the Council and helped draft its Pastoral Constitution on the Church in the Modern World, *Gaudium et Spes*. As a young *peritus* or theological expert at Vatican II, Joseph Ratzinger (the future Pope Benedict XVI) was influential in developing five conciliar texts, including the Council's dogmatic constitutions on the Church and on divine revelation. The papal programs of John Paul II and Benedict XVI were profoundly influenced by their experiences of Vatican II and its reception throughout the world Church. Indeed, their pontificates can be understood as a single, thirty-five-year effort to give the Council an authoritative interpretation. That effort pivoted around the special Synod of 1985, which found the key to interpreting the sixteen documents of Vatican II in the concept of the Church as a communion of disciples in mission. That pivot eventually led to the proclamation of the New Evangelization before and during the Great Jubilee of 2000, and to the 2007 Aparecida Document of the bishops of Latin America and the Caribbean—perhaps the most developed statement yet of what a communion of disciples in mission must be.

Unlike his two papal predecessors, Jorge Mario Bergoglio (the future Pope Francis) did not experience the Second Vatican Council directly. But he was a young Jesuit during the Council and a religious superior in the contentious period immediately following Vatican II. As archbishop of Buenos Aires, he was a crucial figure in drafting the Aparecida Document. As pope, Francis has described Pope Paul VI (who presided over three of Vatican II's four sessions) as his papal model, and he canonized both Pope Paul and Pope John XXIII, the two popes of the Second Vatican Council. Thus Pope Francis is very much a conciliar pope.

The next pope will likely have been a teenager or a very young man during the Vatican II years; he may even have been a child during those years. In any case, he will not have been shaped by the experience of the Council and the immediate debates over its meaning and its reception like John Paul II, Benedict XVI, and Francis. Thus the next pope will be a transitional figure in a different way than his immediate predecessors. So it seems appropriate to ponder now what the Church has learned from its experiences during the pontificates of these three conciliar popes—and to suggest what the next pope might take from that learning.

The Catholic Church will be crossing into uncharted territory in the next pontificate. So it is important to reflect now on two questions:

What has the Holy Spirit been teaching a Church-in-transition?

What are the qualities needed in the man who will lead the Church through this transition, bearing the awesome responsibility and great burden of the Office of Peter, which holds "the keys of the kingdom of heaven" (Mt 16:19)?

The Holy Spirit and This Catholic Moment

"The Father ... will give you another Counselor, to be with you for ever ... the Spirit of truth.... You know him, for he dwells with you, and will be in you."

—John 14:16–17

For the past century and a half, the Holy Spirit has been leading the Catholic Church toward a third millennium of renewed evangelical witness and intensified missionary fervor.

That journey into the depths of the Gospel has been an experience of grace, but it has not been without difficulty. The reforms necessary to ensure that the Church of the twenty-first century can fulfill the Great Commission—"Go ... make disciples of all nations" (Mt 28:19)—remain to be completed. There are deep divisions over Catholic doctrine and identity, Catholic practice, and Catholic mission within the Church itself. The dark shadow of scandal touches many local Churches. Our Catholic moment is not a tranquil one.

Yet if we survey the world Church and note where Catholicism is alive and vital, and where the Church is moribund or dying, the path that the promised Counselor, the Holy Spirit, has set for the Catholic Church in the third millennium comes into focus.

The Church that has embraced the Gospel, offering men and women the great gift of friendship with the Lord Jesus Christ, incorporating those friends of the Lord into the communion of his disciples, and sacramentally empowering those disciples to offer others the gift they have received—*that* Catholicism is alive, even under challenging cultural and political circumstances. And *that* Catholicism is making important contributions to society, culture, and public life.

The Church that has lost confidence in the Gospel, the Church that no longer proclaims the Gospel as saving truth and divine mercy for everyone, the Church that seems to think of itself as a non-governmental organization doing socially approved good works— *that* Catholicism is dying, even where it is financially strong and appears institutionally robust. And *that* Catholicism is quite marginal to society, culture, and public life.

For those with the eyes to see the works of grace, the ears to hear what the Spirit is saying to the Church, and the courage to act on what has been seen and heard, the path forward is thus clear—irrespective of many challenges.

This Spirit-led path toward a Catholicism in which the Church's many institutions become launchpads for mission began almost a century and a half ago.

At his election in 1878, Pope Leo XIII took an evangelically bold decision: Catholicism would leave the defensive bastions it had built during the nineteenth century and engage the modern world in order to convert the modern world; and in doing so, Leo believed, the Church could help build a more solid foundation for modern humanity's aspirations to freedom, prosperity, and solidarity. To realize this vision of an engaged Catholicism, Pope Leo revitalized Catholic intellectual life, urged a new dialogue between the Church and modern science, facilitated the Church's study of its own history, encouraged an intensified Catholic encounter with the Bible, and created modern Catholic social doctrine. During and after Leo's pontificate, this Leonine Revolution caused considerable turbulence within the Church, especially in Europe. The question of just how Catholicism should go about the task of converting the world was sharply and sometimes bitterly debated. Because of that, and thanks to the traumas of history (including two world wars), the path to evangelically centered Catholic renewal was never a smooth one, and walking it always required sacrifice.

Eighty years after Leo became Bishop of Rome, Pope John XXIII was elected. Angelo Giuseppe Roncalli had felt the turbulence created by the Leonine Revolution in his own life and ministry. From his experiences as a papal diplomatic representative in war-torn southeastern Europe, as a postwar papal

nuncio in an exhausted and divided France, and as
cardinal-patriarch of Venice, this close student of history had learned that the Church must move beyond
defending itself against political and cultural aggressors
to embark on a renewed and revitalized mission—
just as one of his heroes, Saint Charles Borromeo,
had done in the sixteenth century when he sat in the
chair of Saint Ambrose in Milan. For at the end of its
second millennium and on the cusp of its third, the
Catholic Church was no longer living in Christendom times, times in which the ambient public culture
helped transmit the faith. It was living, once again, in
apostolic times—times defined by the Great Commission and by a vivid sense of obligation to preach the
Gospel "in season and out of season" (2 Tim 4:2).

John XXIII understood this. And it was to invite
the entire Catholic Church to that understanding of
evangelical imperative and evangelical possibility that
he summoned the Second Vatican Council. Vatican
II would gather the energies set loose by the Leonine
Revolution and focus them through the prism of an
ecumenical council. That council, he hoped, would
be a new experience of Pentecost. And like the first
Christian Pentecost described in the second chapter of
the Acts of the Apostles, that experience of the Holy
Spirit would deepen the Church's faith in the truths
of the Gospel and ignite a vibrant Catholic commitment to evangelization.

John XXIII made clear his intentions for Vatican
II at his opening address to the Council on October

11, 1962, known by the first three words of the Latin text as *Gaudet Mater Ecclesia* (Mother Church Rejoices). When it is remembered at all, that address is remembered today for a single sentence, in which the Pope chided those "prophets of doom" who saw only ruin in modern times.[1] *Gaudet Mater Ecclesia* was far more than an admonition against historical pessimism, however. Throughout his lengthy address, John XXIII returned time and again to a central point: the Church must re-center its self-understanding on Jesus Christ, from whom (as he put it) the Church "takes her name, her grace, and her total meaning".[2] The era of what might be called ecclesiocentricity—a Church often focused in modernity on institutional survival and institutional maintenance—was drawing to a close. A new era of Christocentricity—a Church re-focused on the Gospel proclamation of Jesus Christ as the answer to the question that is every human life—was beginning. That was the direction in which the Holy Spirit had been leading the Church for almost a century. That was the path Catholicism must take into the future, using as platforms from which to convert the world the institutions that had been built and maintained during centuries when the Church was defending itself against hostile powers.

In taking this path, John XXIII insisted, the Catholic Church was not making a sharp break with the past. Rather, it was returning, spiritually and in its religious imagination, to the Galilee of Matthew 28 and the Great Commission. Catholicism was retrieving and renewing its constituting, evangelical purpose. To achieve that purpose—to make disciples of all nations—the Church had to "transmit whole and entire and without distortion" the truths that Christ had bequeathed the first apostolic band, as the Pope put it in *Gaudet Mater Ecclesia*.[3] Yet while he stressed the necessity to safeguard the truths of Catholic faith, Pope John also emphasized the mandate to *transmit*. The Church had to share the gift Christians had been given, so that "the whole of Christian doctrine [might] be more fully and profoundly known".[4] For in those truths, the Pope taught, the men and women of the modern world would better "understand what they themselves really are, what dignity distinguishes them, what goal they must pursue".[5] To preach and witness to the Gospel was to offer humanity the truth about itself—the truth that frees in the deepest meaning of liberation.

The Second Vatican Council was itself a time of contention, and the five and a half decades since its conclusion have been even more contentious. As the third decade of the twenty-first century opens, however, what is most striking is not the postconciliar contentiousness within the Church. Over seventeen hundred years of Catholic history, ecumenical councils were called to deal with contentious issues, often involving fundamental truths of the faith; there were bitter quarrels at ecumenical councils; and ecumenical councils have usually been followed by contention.

There is nothing new about contention in the Catholic Church. It began early on, as we read in the sixth and fifteenth chapters of Acts, and it has continued ever since.

What *is* striking is that, amidst the postconciliar contention that followed Vatican II, those parts of the world Church that embraced the Christ-centered, evangelical vision of the Catholic future that John XXIII proposed in *Gaudet Mater Ecclesia* have flourished. Concurrently, those parts of the world Church that failed to understand that the Counter-Reformation was over and that the Holy Spirit was calling the Church beyond self-maintenance to a vivid sense of mission crumbled under the pressures of the modern world. So did those parts of the world Church that imagined (and that continue to imagine) that the Second Vatican Council marked a radical break with the Catholic past: those who seemed to miss (and continue to miss) John XXIII's call in *Gaudet Mater Ecclesia* for the Church of the future to "transmit whole and entire and without distortion" the truths of the Gospel and the Church's doctrine.

John XXIII's evangelical intention for Vatican II was further underscored by three crucial events in the postconciliar Church. Those moments inspire and animate the living part of the world Church today.

The first of these was Pope Paul VI's 1975 apostolic exhortation, *Evangelii Nuntiandi* (Announcing the Gospel).

Paul VI brought Vatican II to a successful conclusion. But the years immediately following the Council were filled with disagreement over the Council's meaning, by a severe breakdown in Church discipline, and by a Church-shaking explosion of dissent in the wake of Paul's 1968 encyclical on the Catholic ethic of human love (*Humanae Vitae*). As his life was drawing to a close, however, Paul VI wanted to leave the Church what one collaborator called a "pastoral testament".[6] That testament—*Evangelii Nuntiandi*, written to complete the work of the 1974 Synod of Bishops—called the Church back to John XXIII's animating vision for Vatican II.

The pope who took his regnal name from the Apostle to the Gentiles taught that mission is not simply something the Church does; mission is what the Church *is*. And the unique mission of the Catholic Church is the forthright offer of friendship with Jesus Christ: "There is no true evangelization," Paul VI wrote, "if the name, the teaching, the life, the promises, the kingdom, and the mystery of Jesus of Nazareth are not proclaimed".[7] To meet Christ, of course, is to meet the Church, a community that lives by those sacramental sources of grace that enliven faith, hope, and charity. To live in this Church in the most complete sense, the evangelized must become evangelizers. And in becoming evangelists, Pope Paul concluded, Christians also become transformers of culture and society—a transforming work animated by ongoing conversion to Christ.

If *Gaudet Mater Ecclesia* was John XXIII's proposal for the Second Vatican Council's work, *Evangelii Nuntiandi* was Paul VI's summary of that work—and a challenge to move beyond contention to mission.

The second event underscoring the evangelical purpose of Vatican II was the 1985 special session of the Synod of Bishops, called by Pope John Paul II to assess what had gone right and what had gone not-so-right in the implementation of the Council, twenty years after it had been solemnly closed on December 8, 1965.

Unlike previous ecumenical councils, Vatican II did not provide keys to its own authentic interpretation: it defined no doctrine, condemned no heresy, wrote no creed, legislated no laws, commissioned no catechism. The key had to be discovered within the texts of the Council, read through the prism of *Gaudet Mater Ecclesia* and *Evangelii Nuntiandi*. And that "key", the Synod Fathers of 1985 concluded, was the idea of the Church as *a communion of disciples in mission*. Catholicism begins with discipleship, with conversion to and friendship with Jesus Christ—with accepting the Gospel as the truth of the world. That conversion incorporates one into the "communion" of the friends of the Lord Jesus, which is unlike any other set of relationships in its members' lives. And that "communion" does not live for itself alone; it lives to offer others the gift it has been given, friendship with the incarnate Son of God and participation in his Mystical Body, the Church.[8]

The world, and some in the Church, imagined that the post-Vatican II contentions within Catholicism were about power. The Synod of 1985 insisted that what was at stake was the Church's very self-understanding. The center of that self-understanding was, is, and always must be Jesus Christ. And to know the Lord Jesus is to accept the responsibility, individually and as members of the Church, to make him known to others. "Missionary openness for the integral salvation of the world," the Synod Fathers wrote, had once characterized the Church of the New Testament; so must it characterize the Church of Vatican II.[9]

The third event that reinforced the evangelical intention of Vatican II, inspiring the living parts of the world Church in the twenty-first century, was the Great Jubilee of 2000.

John Paul II called the Great Jubilee so that the Church might walk the roads of salvation history again. Why do that? So that, after two millennia, the people of the Church might be reminded that Christianity is not a pious myth. Rather, Christianity rests on certain historical events, things that happened to real men and women, at a certain time in a defined place. And those events, preeminently the encounter with the Risen Lord whom those men and women had first known as the Rabbi Jesus from Nazareth, transformed hitherto timid and marginal people into a communion of disciples that launched a religious revolution.

To drive that point home, John Paul II concluded the Great Jubilee on January 6, 2001, with an apostolic letter, *Novo Millennio Ineunte* (Entering the New Millennium), in which he proposed a biblical metaphor for the Catholicism of the third millennium. As Christ had told the fishermen Peter and Andrew to "put out into the deep" (Lk 5:4) for a catch,[10] so Christ was now calling his Church to leave the shallow, sometimes brackish, seemingly safe waters of institutional management to set out on the turbulent waters of the twenty-first century in order to make a great catch of disciples.

As the Church had begun, so must the Church continue.

This Spirit-led journey through the last decades of the second millennium and the first decades of the third has sometimes been a period of desert-wandering for the Church. There have been moments, occasionally lasting for years, when the journey into a Catholic future defined by the Great Commission has stalled. That is to be expected. A Church composed entirely of the imperfectly converted, a Church of sinners who live by grace and walk by faith, is going to lose its way from time to time. And it may, in those stalled moments, turn in on itself and engage in a kind of fratricidal strife. There have also been moments over the past century and a half when the Church has seemed close to shipwreck. In those moments, it is important to remember that the one divinely inspired book of

Church history, the Acts of the Apostles, ends with a shipwreck—and that seeming catastrophe became the occasion to expand the Church's mission.

Amidst all the difficulties confronting Catholicism—difficulties that typically define the Catholic Church for those who do not know her from the inside—the trajectory of a viable Catholic future remains clear. The Church of the twenty-first century and the third millennium will be a Christ-centered Church, born of the Gospel in full, or it will not be. Those who would lead the Church must understand that. The leaders of the Church must not be frightened by the fact that ours are not Christendom times, but apostolic times. That fact of this Catholic moment ought to be energizing and enlivening, for these are times that call everyone in the Church to the adventure of mission.

Mission is everyone's responsibility in the Church. Leadership in executing that mission can be exercised by many, in different stations of life. Leadership in the work of mission is, however, the defining characteristic of those charged with pastoral authority in the Church. That authority is conferred by the Sacrament of Holy Orders and by communion with the Bishop of Rome.

What is required of the Bishop of Rome in these apostolic times is the subject of these reflections.

The Next Pope and the
New Evangelization

Grace to you and peace from God our Father. We always thank God, the Father of our Lord Jesus Christ, when we pray for you, because we have heard of your faith in Christ Jesus and of the love which you have for all the saints, because of the hope laid up for you in heaven. Of this you have heard before in the word of the truth, the gospel which has come to you, as indeed in the whole world it is bearing fruit and growing.

—Colossians 1:2–6

The next pope must be fully committed to the New Evangelization as the Church's grand strategy in the twenty-first century.

The Dogmatic Constitution on the Church, known by its Latin title as *Lumen Gentium* (The Light of the Nations), and the Dogmatic Constitution on Divine Revelation, *Dei Verbum* (The Word of God), were the two most important documents produced by the Second Vatican Council. In them, the Council Fathers located the *fact* of the Catholic Church within

the vast panorama of salvation history. That historical perspective and the understanding of the Church
that flows from it are essential to authentic Catholic
reform and revitalized Catholic mission, including the
mission of the Office of Peter.

According to *Lumen Gentium* and *Dei Verbum*, God
unfolded a design of redemption and sanctification
from his very creation of the universe. First made
explicitly known through God's self-revelation to the
people of Israel, that design was brought to fulfillment
in the life, death, and Resurrection of Jesus of Nazareth, the incarnate Son of God. In his person, the Lord
Jesus inaugurated the Kingdom of God in history (as
he himself announced in Mark 1:15: "The kingdom
of God is at hand; repent, and believe in the gospel").
And by doing so, the Lord empowered those who
believe in him, and who accept his offer of friendship,
to live beyond history, here and now, in the communion of disciples that is the Church. Thus the Church
is because of what *Lumen Gentium* described as the
"utterly gratuitous and mysterious design of [divine]
wisdom and goodness", which was intended from
the beginning to "raise up men to share in ... [the]
divine life".[1]

And at the center of the fact of the Church is the
fact of Jesus Christ.

Salvation history does not run parallel to world history. Salvation history *is* world history read in its
true depth and against its proper horizon. Thus the

Church does not stand outside history but within history, reminding the world of the deepest truth about itself. And if the Church is an expression and an integral part of God's plan for the salvation of the world, then the Church is not a historical accident (like so many other institutions that arise, exist for a time, and then disappear). So the Church cannot be understood in sociological terms alone. That is why the Council Fathers of Vatican II urged all Catholics to think of the Church in images drawn from the Bible, the written Word of God. At moments when the human failings of the people of the Church and its leaders are all too obvious, when the institutional Church is held in contempt by some and evangelical energies wane in the face of a host of crises and challenges, it is important to remember the deeper truths about the Church that these biblical metaphors convey.

According to *Lumen Gentium*, the Church is the "sheepfold, the sole and necessary gateway to which is Christ (John 10:1–10)."[2] The Church is also the "flock, of which God foretold that he would himself be the shepherd (Isaiah 40:11; Exodus 34:11ff.)."[3] And the sheep of that flock "are ... at all times led and brought to pasture by Christ himself, the Good Shepherd and prince of shepherds (cf. John 10:11; 1 Peter 5:4), who gave his life for his sheep (cf. John 10:11–16)."[4]

The Church is also the vineyard that "has been planted by the heavenly cultivator (Matthew 21:33–43; cf. Isaiah 5:1ff.)."[5] And in that vineyard, "the true vine is Christ, who gives life and fruitfulness to the branches, that is ... to us, who through the Church remain in Christ without whom we can do nothing (John 15:1–5)."[6]

The living parts of the Catholic Church today are those animated by the conviction that Jesus Christ, the incarnate Son of God, is the center of the Church. The living parts of the Catholic Church today are those that have given themselves, in the words of *Lumen Gentium*, to "Christ, who is the light of the world, from whom we go forth, through whom we live, and towards whom our whole life is directed".[7]

The Catholic Church does not exist by itself or for itself. The Catholic Church exists because of the salvific design of God, which is the interior truth of history and the cosmos. And the Catholic Church exists to proclaim Jesus Christ and his Gospel.

R e-centering the Church on Christ and the Gospel was one of the great accomplishments of the Spirit-led movement of Catholic renewal that began in the pontificate of Pope Leo XIII. Re-centering the Church on Christ and the Gospel was one of Pope John XXIII's intentions for the Second Vatican Council. It was to remind the Church of this Spirit-led dynamic and this intention that Pope Paul VI wrote *Evangelii Nuntiandi*, that the Fathers of the special Synod of 1985 summed up the Council's concept of the Church as a communion of disciples in mission, and that Pope John Paul II called the Church to go "into the deep" of the New Evangelization in *Novo Millenno Ineunte.*

Thus it cannot be said too often, although it must often be said because the tendency to think of the Church in institutional terms is so deeply ingrained in the Catholic imagination: Jesus Christ and his Gospel are the reason the Church *is.* And because of that, the proclamation of that Gospel and that Christ must be at the center of what the Catholic Church *does.*

The Catholic Church does many things, of course. The Church worships the one true God "in spirit and truth" (Jn 4:23). As the Fathers of Vatican II wrote in the Constitution on the Sacred Liturgy (*Sacrosanctum Concilium*), "it is the liturgy through which, especially in the divine sacrifice of the Eucharist, 'the work of our salvation is accomplished', and it is through the liturgy, especially, that the faithful are enabled to express in their lives and manifest to others the mystery of Christ and the real nature of the true Church."[8]

The Church binds up wounds, proclaims liberty to captives, defends the defenseless, empowers the poor, educates those yearning for knowledge, comforts the sick, and buries the dead. In its many works of charity, education, and mercy, the Catholic Church enriches the lives of millions who are not Catholics but whom the Church nevertheless believes are men and women of inalienable dignity and value for whom the Son of God suffered and died. In those works, the

Church can and does draw others to Christ and to the communion of his friends.

Yet all these things the Church *does* flow from the basic truth of what the Church *is* and must be: the herald of the Gospel. The Church worships in spirit and in truth because God is to be worshipped; because Christ commanded his friends to celebrate the Eucharist of the New Covenant "in remembrance of me" (Lk 22:19); because worship in spirit and truth deepens the Christian's understanding of his or her baptismal dignity; and because the grace of sacramental worship equips the friends of Jesus Christ for mission. The Church does good works, not because this wins the Church the world's approval, but because Christ the Lord commanded his friends to do these things—and because doing them often helps unbelievers feel the warming flame of divine love for the first time.

Above all, however, the Lord Jesus commanded his friends to preach the Gospel and thereby share with others the gift they had been given.

Thus everything in the Church and everyone in the Church is subordinate to the Gospel. Those who do not subordinate themselves to the Gospel place themselves in a defective state of communion with the Church and with Christ.

The Gospel cannot be proclaimed unless the Gospel is embraced as *true*. The Fathers of both the First and Second Vatican Councils understood this.

In its Dogmatic Constitution on the Catholic Faith, *Dei Filius* (The Son of God), the bishops of Vatican I made two crucial affirmations in 1870: that the reality of God can be known by the light of reason, and that there are attributes of God that can only be known by revelation. This dual affirmation of faith and reason as pathways to knowledge of God has been critical to maintaining the integrity of Catholic faith under contemporary cultural conditions, in which the human capacity to grasp the truth of anything with certainty is often questioned. Thus John Paul II, in his 1998 encyclical *Fides et Ratio*, taught that the "faith and reason" of his encyclical's title are like two wings on which the human spirit ascends to the contemplation of truth.[9] Pope Benedict XVI taught on many occasions that reason is essential in order to purify faith from superstition, while faith prevents reason from closing in upon itself and surrendering to a positivistic materialism that reduces the human person to congealed cosmic dust.

Confronted by an even more skeptical and secularized world than the Fathers of Vatican I, the Fathers of the Second Vatican Council insisted just as strongly on the truth of divine revelation. At Vatican II, many bishops, especially those from a Europe morally and culturally shattered by three totalitarian systems and two world wars, knew that the mid-twentieth century was being experienced as a time of disturbing silence—a silence that seemed to suggest a cosmos without meaning. In the face of what many

culture-shapers experienced as emptiness, the bishops of the Second Vatican Council insisted God had
broken through the silence: that God had spoken to
humanity in the past and that God continues to speak
to humanity in the present. God broke through the
silence, first by revealing himself by word and deed to
his people, Israel. Later, God spoke a definitive word
into history by revealing himself in the person of the
Son, the second Person of the Trinity, incarnate as
Jesus of Nazareth, the son of Mary as well as the Son
of God.

In the decades prior to Vatican II, Catholic theo-
logians debated with their Protestant academic
colleagues a question that arose in the various Reformations of the sixteenth century: Is there one
"source" of divine revelation, Scripture, or were there
two sources, Scripture and Tradition? The Fathers of
Vatican II taught that the one "source" of revelation
is God himself, who spoke to humanity through both
Sacred Scripture and Sacred Tradition, and who, in
speaking to humanity, spoke truths that were true for
all time and in all places, and thus binding in all times
and all places.

At this moment in Catholic history, in which some
deny that God's revelation judges history and suggest that the flow of history and our present experience judge the truths of revelation, it is important to
remember how robust the Second Vatican Council's
defense of the reality and the truth of divine revelation

was. Here is what the Council Fathers wrote in the second chapter of *Dei Verbum*:

> God graciously arranged that the things he had once revealed for the salvation of all peoples should remain in their entirety, throughout the ages, and be transmitted to all generations. Therefore, Christ the Lord, in whom the entire Revelation of the most high God is summed up (cf. 2 Corinthians 1:20; 3:16–4:6), commanded the apostles to preach the Gospel, which had been promised beforehand by the Prophets, and which he fulfilled in his own person and promulgated with his own lips. In preaching the Gospel they were to communicate the gifts of God to all men. This Gospel was to be the source of all saving truth and moral discipline. This was faithfully done: it was done by the apostles who handed on, by the spoken word of their preaching, by the example they gave, by the institutions they established, what they themselves had received—whether from the lips of Christ, from his way of life and his works, or whether they had learned it at the prompting of the Holy Spirit; it was done by these apostles and other men associated with the apostles who, under the inspiration of the same Holy Spirit, committed the message of salvation to writing....
>
> Sacred Tradition and sacred Scripture, then, are bound closely together, and communicate with one another. For both of them, flowing from the same divine well-spring, come together in some fashion to form one thing, and move towards the same goal. Sacred Scripture is the speech of God as it is put down

in writing under the breath of the Holy Spirit. And Tradition transmits in its entirety the Word of God which has been entrusted to the apostles by Christ the Lord and the Holy Spirit....

Sacred Tradition and sacred Scripture make up a single sacred deposit of the Word of God, which is entrusted to the Church.[10]

Lumen Gentium and *Dei Verbum*, the two foundational texts of the Second Vatican Council, must therefore be read together. The Church cannot properly understand itself, nor can it properly order its life and mission, without supernatural faith in divine revelation. The Church manifests that faith through preaching the Scriptures as the Word of God and by obedience to those truths taught by the Church's magisterium as permanent features of the Church's Tradition.

The next pope must understand this and teach it to the entire world Church.

Many recent debates in the Catholic Church, including the debates before, during, and after the Synods of 2014, 2015, and 2018, and during the 2019 special Synod on Amazonia, were, at bottom, debates about the reality and binding force of revelation. Do the words of the Lord Jesus on the nature of marriage and its permanence remain true and binding for today? Or does our experience of the fragility of marriage in contemporary society empower us to adjust or even correct what Jesus taught? Do the words and injunctions of Saint Paul on worthiness to receive Holy Communion remain true and binding for today? Or has our historical moment empowered us to adjust or correct what Saint Paul taught? Do the teachings of the Lord Jesus and Saint Paul on the ethics of human love, and what makes for a love that fosters happiness and beatitude, remain true and binding for today? Or has the sexual revolution empowered us to see more clearly on these matters than the Lord Jesus, Saint Paul, and the consistent teaching of the Church for two millennia? Does the Great Commission to go and make disciples of all nations apply to indigenous peoples?

These and similar debates are not about "policy". They are about the reality of divine revelation. And it is important to note that these debates typically emerge from specific sociological and historical locations.

In the main, those arguing that history judges revelation, such that the Church can, so to speak, improve on what was taught by the Lord Jesus and the Apostle to the Gentiles, come from older local Churches that have felt the full brunt of the cultural assault on Catholicism that began in the continental Enlightenments of the nineteenth century—Catholic communities, especially in the German-speaking lands, whose liberal Protestant neighbors long ago bade farewell to the notion of a divine revelation that is binding over time. This sociological and historical fact invites the conclusion (however reluctant some may be to draw it) that what is really at work when churchmen propose adjusting revelation to fit a contemporary cultural template is a lack of faith in the Son of God, a lack of conviction about the possibility of proclaiming the Lord Jesus as the Son of God, and thus a failure to offer friendship with Jesus Christ as the answer to the deepest longings of the human heart. Surrender to the surrounding cultural mores follows in short order. So does a strained attempt to "baptize" those mores, as it were. So do efforts, tacit or explicit, to reconfigure the Church as a voluntary organization doing good works in society.

By contrast, the strongest defense of the reality and binding authority of revelation in recent Catholic debates has come from the younger local Churches of Africa and from those parts of the Church in the West that are living the New Evangelization as the Church's grand strategy for the twenty-first century and the third millennium. Where faith in Christ is strong and where that faith is eagerly proclaimed as truly liberating, the truths of revelation appear to be the Magna Carta of human happiness: the pathway to the knowledge of God and to eternal life. And from that proclamation of the truth of God in Christ, true service to society follows.

The Catholic Church of the New Evangelization— which is the Catholic Church of the truth of revelation—lives. The Catholic Church of cultural accommodation—the Church uncertain about the truth of revelation and therefore incapable of proclaiming the Gospel fearlessly—is dying or dead.

The next pope must understand this.

These empirical facts of Catholicism's twenty-first-century situation underscore the truth of what *Lumen Gentium* and the Fathers of Vatican II taught: the Church—centered on Christ "from whom we go forth, through whom we live, and towards whom our whole life is directed"[11]—is a sacramental community of grace in which all are called to be heralds of the Gospel. Put another way, the Catholic Church is not another NGO (non-governmental organization), like many other institutions on the world stage.

NGOs do important work in a variety of fields. The history of the twentieth century is a powerful reminder that a healthy civil society, in which non-governmental organizations and natural human communities like the family flourish, is essential to freedom, prosperity, and solidarity. The alternative is the flattened social landscape of totalitarianism, with its attendant tyranny.

But the Catholic Church cannot think of itself as an NGO. When it does so, its evangelical arteries are hardened, even when it controls considerable financial resources and deploys a large bureaucratic infrastructure. The more tolerant sectors of postmodern Western culture are prepared to live with the Catholic Church as an NGO, and in fact often push the Church in that direction. What postmodern Western culture finds increasingly hard to tolerate is a Catholic Church that, without aggression but also without apology, proclaims Jesus Christ as Lord and Savior and his Gospel as the truth of the world. Under this cultural (and political and legal) pressure, Catholics who have lost confidence in the Gospel's power to change lives have been tempted to reduce the Church to an NGO—and have too often succumbed to that temptation. To do so, however, is to manifest a lack of faith in the Gospel, which Saint Paul proclaimed in Romans 1:16 as "the power of God for salvation to every one who has faith".

The most important debate in the Catholic Church in the third decade of the twenty-first century is not the argument over whether the Second Vatican Council was a wise idea or a foolish idea. That debate can only be engaged seriously several hundred years from now. Then, it will have become clearer whether Vatican II was a reprise of the Fifth Lateran Council, a reforming council of the early sixteenth century that failed to reenergize the Church for evangelization and mission, or a reprise of the Council of Trent, a reforming council that succeeded in renewing the Church according to the truths of the Gospel, resulting in a great explosion of missionary energy.

The most important debate in the Catholic Church today is one that began during the last two sessions of Vatican II in 1964 and 1965 and that has continued ever since: the debate over whether Vatican II was a council in continuity with revelation and tradition, or a council of rupture and discontinuity in which the Church essentially reinvented itself.

The texts of Vatican II demonstrate that the Council Fathers accepted both John XXIII's admonition to preserve intact the fullness of Catholic faith *and* his challenge to devise ways to express that faith so that it could be heard by the people of today. The living parts of the Catholic Church are those that followed that path of renewal in continuity with revelation and tradition. The dying parts of the Church are those which insist that Vatican II represented a "paradigm shift"—as if something happened in the Catholic Church between October 11, 1962, and December 8, 1965, that was the equivalent of what happened when Copernicus demonstrated that the Earth is not the center of the solar system, but rather revolves around the Sun. That shift—from Ptolemaic cosmology to Copernican cosmology—was a true "paradigm shift", a radical break with the past and the start of a different path into the future.

The Catholic Church does not do paradigm shifts, because Jesus Christ—"the same yesterday and today and for ever" (Heb 13:8)—is *always* the center of the Church. There is no evangelization that does not begin with that conviction. Nor is there a Catholic future.

The next pope must grasp all this and must be committed to leading a Christ-centered Church in the work of evangelization. The next pope must manifest the power of the Gospel in his own life. And the next pope must understand that the work of evangelization succeeds only when the Gospel is offered in full. That offer must be made with complete respect for human freedom and with a compassionate understanding of those complexities of the human heart of which the prophet Jeremiah wrote some twenty-six hundred years ago. But the offer of the Gospel, in full, must be made.

The Next Pope and the Office of Peter

*"Simon, Simon, . . . I have prayed for you that your
faith may not fail; and when you have turned again,
strengthen your brethren. "*

—Luke 22:32

*The next pope must have a firm grasp on
the nature of the Petrine Office and its roles
in the Church of the New Evangelization.*

Like everything else in the Church, the Office of
Peter—the unique ministry exercised by the Bishop
of Rome—is at the service of the Gospel and its
proclamation. At the Mass publicly inaugurating his
Petrine ministry in 1978, Pope John Paul II offered
a memorable lesson in this ancient truth. Its echoes
continue to reverberate throughout the living parts of
world Catholicism.

On October 22, 1978, the Church was still in shock
over the unexpected death of Pope John Paul I after a
thirty-three day papacy. The world was skeptical, at
best, about the possibility of papal leadership. The
Roman Curia was stunned by the election of the first

non-Italian pope in 455 years. Yet by the end of the papal Mass that day, the world, the Church, and the Curia knew that something had changed, and changed dramatically. French journalist André Frossard captured the character of the moment when he wrote back to his Paris-based newspaper, "This is not a pope from Poland; this is a pope from Galilee."

What did John Paul II do over the course of three hours?

He displayed the power of the Gospel in his own life, affirming without hesitation that Jesus Christ is the Lord who uniquely knows and satisfies the deepest longings of the human heart. Thus the first words of his homily, delivered outdoors before a vast throng in St. Peter's Square and before millions on television, were a bold repetition of Simon Peter's confession of faith at Caesarea Philippi: "You are the Christ, the Son of the living God" (Mt 16:16). That, he said, was the divinely inspired profession of faith from which the Office of Peter was born.

He proclaimed the power of the Gospel to reveal both the face of God the merciful Father and the greatness of our humanity. For Christ, he said, had brought humanity close "to the mystery of the living God" even as Christ had shown us "the ultimate and definitive truth" about ourselves.[1] And that, he taught, is what the Church must propose to the world: "Please, listen once again," he asked.

He explained the power of the Gospel by reminding the Church and the world that the Gospel is the only power the Church possesses, and that "the mystery of the Cross and Resurrection" is the only power the Church should want: "the absolute and yet sweet and gentle power of the Lord", a power that "responds to the whole depths of the human person, to his loftiest aspirations of intellect, heart, and soul".[2]

He embodied the power of the Gospel by reminding the Church that Catholic leadership is a leadership of service by the will of Christ. That was what Christ had taught the apostles by washing their feet at the Last Supper (see Jn 13:1–20), and that was what Christ was teaching the bishops and the pope today. And so he prayed, before the world and the Church, "Christ, make me become and remain the servant of your unique power, the servant of your sweet power, the servant of your power that knows no eventide. Make me a servant. Indeed, the servant of your servants."[3]

He challenged the world to experience the power of the Gospel, and in doing so to rid itself of the fears that closed hearts and minds to God: "Do not be afraid! Be not afraid to welcome Christ and accept his power. Help [me] and all those who wish to serve Christ and with Christ's power to serve the human person and the whole of mankind. Be not afraid! Open wide the doors for Christ. To his saving power open the boundaries of states, economic, and political systems, the vast fields of culture, civilization, and development. Be not afraid."[4]

Two decades later, in closing the Great Jubilee of 2000, that same "pope from Galilee" would urge the

Church to "put out into the deep" of the New Evangelization. That valedictory command from Peter's
263rd successor was implicit in John Paul II's first
public papal homily. By retrieving a Galilean experience, it set the pattern for the Church's mission in the
twenty-first century and the third millennium.

While Canon 1404 in the Church's legal code
states that "the First See is judged by no one,"
the pope, the Bishop of Rome who leads the First
See as Successor of Peter, is not above the Gospel or
the Church. Nor can Peter's Office in the Church be
understood by analogy to an absolutist czar or dictator.

As the Second Vatican Council was concluding its
work on the Dogmatic Constitution on the Church,
Pope Paul VI proposed that *Lumen Gentium* include a
sentence asserting that the pope "is accountable to the
Lord alone".[5] The Council's Theological Commission, which included some very old-fashioned theo-
logians, rejected that formula. The Commission noted
that "the Roman Pontiff is also bound to revelation
itself, to the fundamental structure of the Church, to
the sacraments, to the definitions of earlier Councils,
and other obligations too numerous to mention."[6]
Thus it is a serious mistake to imagine the papacy as an
authoritarian office from which the pope issues impe-
rious decisions that reflect his will alone. Rather, the
Petrine Office is an *authoritative* office whose holder
is the custodian of an *authoritative* tradition. He is the
servant of that tradition, that body of doctrine and
practice, not its master.

Recognizing both the vast authority of his office and the boundaries within which that authority must be exercised is a challenge for any pope, and will be for the next pope. One way to meet that challenge is for the next pope to welcome and respond to serious, respectful questions and critique from those who share concern for and responsibility for the Church—and especially from the pope's brother bishops who, when necessary, must summon the courage to do for Peter what Paul did for him, as Paul testified in Galatians 2:11: offer him fraternal correction.

In the twenty-first chapter of John's Gospel, the Risen Lord three times challenges Peter: "Do you love me more than these? ... Do you love me? ... Do you love me?" (vv. 15–17). It is tempting to see here a riposte to Peter's three denials after Jesus was arrested: having denied his Lord three times, Peter must now profess his faith three times. A deeper reading of that encounter suggests something else—Peter is being asked whether he can empty himself of himself "more than these" (i.e., the rest), in order to tend the Lord's flock as its chief shepherd. All those ordained as priests and bishops in the Catholic Church are asked to empty themselves of themselves in order to be Christ for the Church and the world. That Johannine Gospel vignette suggests that it is in the nature of the Petrine Office that the pope must empty himself more fully than the rest. In order to exercise his ministry as the universal "servant of the servants of God" (a papal title that began with Pope Saint Gregory the Great),

Peter's Successor must open himself to the working of divine grace in his life so that he can empty himself of himself as much as is humanly possible.

That self-emptying touches on another facet of the papacy, the pope assuming a new name.

The tradition of the pope taking a new name began when the Roman priest Mercury, on his election as Bishop of Rome in 533, decided that a pope with the name of a pagan god would not do; so Mercury adopted the regnal name "John II" in honor of a papal martyr. Like the story of Jesus and Peter on the Galilean lakeshore, however, this tradition has a deeper meaning. The assumption of a regnal name symbolizes the fact that the Bishop of Rome, as universal pastor of the Church, no longer belongs to himself, to the diocese he once led or the religious community to which he previously belonged, or to a particular country.

These truths of the Petrine Office, disclosed by Scripture and Tradition, carry several implications that the next pope must grasp.

To demonstrate that he is responsible to no earthly sovereignty but is a sovereign in his own right, the next pope should return his passport and other national identity documents to the public authorities of his country of origin, immediately after his election. For over a century, Vatican diplomacy worked tenaciously to ensure that the Petrine Office was independent of mundane powers; popes must conduct themselves in such a way as to reinforce that point.

Similarly, and even in his personal pastoral work, the pope cannot detach himself from his office, as if there were "Pope X" here and "Father Y" there. As long as a man holds the Office of Peter, he is only "Pope X".

The uniqueness of the Petrine Office also places strong demands on the self-discipline of the man who holds it. Thus the next pope must take care not to speak in such a way as to identify his personal opinions with the settled teaching of the Church. A papal sense of humor is entirely welcome; so is a self-disciplining commitment to papal decorum.

John Paul II and his spokesman, Joaquín Navarro-Valls, demonstrated that what Navarro called the "dialectic" between the Office of Peter and the press could help advance the Church's evangelical mission. With sufficient hard work and skill, it is possible for the Holy See Press Office to amplify the Bishop of Rome's voice, so that he can, as he must by the Lord's command, "strengthen [the] brethren" (Lk 22:32). This interaction, however, should always be for evangelical and pastoral purposes. In his interactions with the media, the next pope should therefore take care always to point beyond himself, to Christ and the Gospel, rather than toward himself. Papal press conferences can be useful, in theory; but the danger of papal press conferences reinforcing stereotypes of the Bishop of Rome as the supermanager of an international NGO must be weighed carefully by the next pope. Moreover, in the twenty-first-century media (and social media) environment, the pope can become a declining asset to the New Evangelization if he speaks so often as to blunt the impact of what is really important for the Bishop of Rome, the "first witness" to the Gospel and its power, to say. The same diminishment of witness can happen when a pope speaks so harshly of others as to lessen his own Christian dignity as well as the dignity of those whom he criticizes.

As the Church's "first witness", the pope must also take care that his unique witness not be confused with the agendas of those who wish to co-opt the authority and image of the Petrine Office for their own purposes. Papal self-discipline in this respect is particularly important in a social media/internet age, in which it is relatively easy for social activists or politicians to use a quick papal selfie for their own purposes—which may not be the Church's purposes, or the Gospel's. The imperative of papal self-discipline also suggests ending arrangements by which journalistic entities are permitted to claim that they are "reflecting the mind of the Vatican". Only the pope and his official press representative should make that claim, for only they can make it authoritatively.

None of this is to suggest that the next pope and his successors should disappear from public view save on important liturgical or ceremonial occasions. It is to suggest that a deeper reflection on the relationship between the pope's public presence (including his media presence) and the New Evangelization is required.

Then there is the question of papal residence. Popes have lived in different venues over the centuries: the Lateran Palace (which now houses the officers of the Diocese of Rome); the Quirinale (now home to the president of Italy); the Apostolic Palace, in the Vatican; and the Vatican guesthouse known as the Domus Sanctae Marthae. Mythologies (and movies) notwithstanding, the papal apartments in the Apostolic Palace are not replete with Renaissance grandeur; they are like many other middle-class Italian homes. Where the pope lives, however, is of less consequence than *how* the pope lives: Does he live in conversation with a broad range of personalities or not?

To be the Church's "first witness", the pope must be informed about the wide variety of situations faced by local Churches. It is also useful in exercising his office if he has a broad familiarity with his people and their pastors. As the Church has grown to a communion of more than a billion souls, the complexities of the information a pope must absorb in order to know how to "strengthen the brethren" have increased exponentially. No man can know all that a pope needs to know, of course, and that is why the pope has a staff, the Roman Curia. Still, the universality of the pope's pastorate means that he must have some familiarity with many different ecclesiastical environments, in order to be an effective pastor for the world Church. Thus he must be in regular contact with those who will tell him what in conscience they think he needs to know.

The pope will always be a man of a certain background and formation, which will shape how he conducts his papal ministry. But a pope who relies too heavily, even exclusively, on his own pre-papal knowledge will be less likely to function well in the Petrine Office. A pope who relies too heavily or even exclusively on information from "inside" sources like the papal diplomatic service and the Roman Curia—where information is typically perceived and transmitted through familiar bureaucratic grooves—will be similarly disabled. Pope Pius XI, a crusty personality who did not disdain to deploy the monarchical plural, was said to have burst out in exasperation once, "Must we spend our life listening to things we already know?" The exasperation aside, that thirst for knowing more is essential to a papacy that advances the New Evangelization.

The next pope must work to strengthen the unity of the Church at a moment when that unity is threatened by centrifugal forces in the ambient public culture of the West and inside the Church itself.

Ever since Pope Paul VI established the world Synod of Bishops with the 1965 apostolic letter *Apostolica Sollicitudo* (Apostolic Concern), the Church has debated the meaning of "synodality". In the Eastern Catholic Churches, "synodality" has a specific meaning based on a distinctive history and refers to the way in which the bishops of those Churches govern. "Synodality" is a relatively new concept in Latin-Rite

Catholicism, however. Finding its true meaning and appropriate expression has not been easy over the past half-century. It seems likely that the discussion over what synodality means in the universal Church will continue for some time.

The next pope must define, and thereby clarify, the boundaries of that discussion.

Whatever else "synodality" may mean, it does not and cannot mean that the Catholic Church is a global federation of local Churches, each of which lays legitimate claim to a distinctive doctrinal, moral, and pastoral profile. That is Anglicanism, not Catholicism. And the disastrous results of this kind of local-option Christianity in the Anglican Communion should give pause to any Catholic—and certainly any pope—who imagines that the dramatic "decentralization" of doctrinal and moral authority in the Church is pastorally effective or evangelically fruitful.

Many currents in contemporary culture, especially in the West, work as centrifugal forces, spinning local Churches off into their own ecclesial orbits. This is most obvious in the German-speaking Catholic world in the twenty-first century, but the phenomenon is not limited to Germany, Austria, and the German-speaking parts of Switzerland. Thus the next pope must strive to reinforce the Church's unity by teaching and governing in such a way as to underscore the theological priority of the universal Church in the Catholic Church's self-understanding. This will mean, among other things, that no papal decision affecting the entire

Church will be made on the basis of specific local situations, and that the world Church will be consulted
on matters affecting all.

Concurrently, the next pope must call wayward
local Churches, whose concern for the unique situations they face has led them into de facto states of
apostasy or schism, into a renewed and reformed relationship to the universal Church, its doctrine, and its
pastoral practice.

That the pope is the Church's first witness to Christ
and the Gospel is, according to Catholic teaching, of the will of Christ. It was also Christ's will that
all of his disciples be witnesses and that all be evangelists. That means that, while the pope is the Church's
first witness, he is not the Church's only witness. And
his responsibilities include doing everything he can
to encourage others to fulfill their responsibilities as
witnesses to the Gospel and its power.

Today, the pope and the papacy are at the center
of the Catholic imagination. That was not always the
case. Prior to Pope Pius IX, who served as Bishop of
Rome from 1846 until 1878, most Catholics had little
idea who "the pope" was, much less what the pope
said or did. Thanks to the development of the popular
press, to the travails he suffered while the Papal States
were being stripped away by the new Kingdom of
Italy, to the number of jubilees he celebrated during
his lengthy pontificate (which brought throngs of pil-
grims to Rome), and to the drama of the First Vatican

Council, Pius IX became a real personality to many of
the world's Catholics—the first pope whose picture
Catholics displayed in their homes. Most Catholics
were unaware of the theological fine points embedded
in Vatican I's carefully crafted affirmation that, under
certain defined conditions, the pope could teach infallibly on matters of faith and morals. But in Pius IX,
Catholics knew they had a pope. And from Pius IX
on, the pope and the papacy grew ever larger in both
the Catholic imagination and the world's thinking
about the Church.

This "papal protagonism", as some have described
it, has helped the Church unleash the power of the
Gospel on more than one occasion. It was one reason why Pope Pius X could swiftly reconfigure the
spiritual landscape of Catholicism by admitting seven-
year-old children to Holy Communion, that Pope
Pius XI could extend and deepen Pope Leo XIII's
social doctrine while challenging three totalitarian ideologies, and that Pope Pius XII could set the intellectual stage for the Second Vatican Council with the
1943 encyclicals *Mystici Corporis Christi* (The Mystical
Body of Christ) and *Divino Afflante Spiritu* (Inspired
by the Holy Spirit), and the 1947 encyclical *Mediator
Dei* (The Mediator between God and Man). "Papal
protagonism" has had its effects in world history, too,
most notably in John Paul II's pivotal role in igniting
the revolution of conscience that helped make possible
the nonviolent political Revolution of 1989 and the
collapse of European communism.

"Papal protagonism"—the Office of Peter at the very center of the Catholic imagination—has also had less happy effects in the Church.

If bishops think of the pope as the center of all initiative in the Church, they may be less eager to take the responsibility they have for unleashing the power of the Gospel in their people.

If bishops and superiors of religious communities interpret "papal protagonism" to mean that they need not take necessary disciplinary action for the good of their dioceses or communities because "Rome will fix it", those local Churches and communities suffer—and so does the entire Church.

"Papal protagonism" can also have the unhappy effect of suggesting—not least through the media and social media—that what the pope does and says sums up the meaning, work, and condition of the Catholic Church at any given moment in time. This is simply not true. And it can distract attention from the growing parts of the world Church where the power of the Gospel is being unleashed. How many Catholics, and how much of the world media, have missed the phenomenal growth of Catholicism in sub-Saharan Africa in the post-Vatican II years, missing that extraordinary flowering of the Gospel because of a too-tight focus on the papacy and the controversies surrounding it? How many Catholics today are sadly unaware of the many good things happening in their own local Church and throughout the world Church because they are spellbound by the papacy and fixated on what the pope says and does?

The next pope must rebalance the position of the papacy in the life of the twenty-first-century Church. The pope must and will remain the Church's supreme authority. That authority, however, must be exercised in such a way that it facilitates the leadership of others, especially the Church's bishops. And the supreme authority must demand, when necessary, that local authorities discharge their responsibilities so that the power of the Gospel may be visible in all the people of the Church.

This will be less a matter of "shrinking" the papacy than of the papacy empowering the missionary discipleship of others. Given the unique structure of authority in the Catholic Church, a measure of "papal protagonism" is not only inevitable but desirable. If the pope understands that strengthening the brethren is one essential responsibility of his office, however, he will exercise his office in a way that points beyond himself to Christ. And he will lead in ways that remind his flock that they are all missionary disciples, called to witness to the power of the Gospel and to make Christ known to the world.

That is the Petrine Office in service to the New Evangelization.

The Next Pope and the Fullness of Catholic Faith

"If you continue in my word, you are truly my disciples, and you will know the truth, and the truth will make you free."

—John 8:31–32

The next pope must understand that doctrine is liberating and that Catholicism can and must be both a Church of doctrinal clarity and a Church manifesting the divine mercy.

There seems to be a kind of iron law built into the relationship between Christianity and modernity (and late modernity, and postmodernity, and probably whatever is coming after postmodernity): Christian communities that have a clear sense of doctrinal and moral identity can survive and even flourish under the challenges posed by contemporary culture; Christian communities whose sense of identity becomes weak and whose boundaries become porous wither—and some die.

This iron law was first demonstrated among the various forms of liberal Protestantism around the world.

The liberal Protestant denominations that began abandoning doctrinal clarity in the nineteenth century and moral clarity in the twentieth are dying, everywhere. The growing end of Protestantism throughout the world is evangelical, Pentecostal, or fundamentalist. And while there are vast differences in theological sensibility and pastoral method among evangelical Protestants, Pentecostalists, and Protestant fundamentalists, each of these forms of Christianity exhibits clarity of teaching and strong moral expectations.

The iron law is also applicable to world Catholicism.

There is a strong correlation between the collapse of Catholic belief and practice in Western Europe and the ongoing attempt there to make "Catholic Lite"—a Catholicism of indeterminate convictions and porous behavioral boundaries—work as a twenty-first-century pastoral method. This phenomenon is most obvious in the German-speaking lands of Europe, but it is not confined there. Catholic Lite is an evangelical and pastoral failure throughout Western Europe, as it is an evangelical and pastoral failure in North America, Latin America, Australia, and New Zealand.

By contrast, the living, vibrant parts of the world Church in the third decade of the twenty-first century are those that have made the proclamation of the Gospel their priority; that teach the Catholic faith in full, with imagination and compassion; and that offer fallen-away Catholics, dissatisfied Protestants, and unbelievers a reformed and more satisfying way of life, rooted in friendship with the Lord Jesus Christ. This is most obviously true of the newer local Churches of sub-Saharan Africa. It is also true of the growing end of the Church in North America. And it is true of those shoots of new Christian life that are sprouting up through the hard, secularized soil of Europe.

This basic truth of twenty-first-century Catholic life—Catholicism-in-full is attractive and compelling; Catholic Lite is moribund—also extends across a range of Catholic institutions. It is true of parishes, dioceses, religious communities, seminaries, and lay renewal movements. Perhaps the most dramatic example is found in communities of women religious in the West. There, communities that have abandoned the religious habit and a distinctive mode of life, and whose members regularly dissent from authoritative Church teaching, are dying; those that have embraced the reform of religious life mandated by the Second Vatican Council in the decree *Perfectae Caritatis* (Perfect Charity) as authoritatively interpreted by Pope John Paul II in the 1996 apostolic exhortation *Vita Consecrata* (The Consecrated Life) are growing—even as society makes more and more opportunities for service and leadership available to women. Lay renewal movements in the Church follow a similar pattern: those that have flourished in the past several decades embrace Catholicism-in-full.

That Catholicism-in-full attracts is also demonstrated by the remarkable fact that, in the United States, seminary recruitment has not collapsed under the pressure of the scandal of clerical sexual abuse. A young man discerning a priestly vocation today is not only considering a challenging way to live his Catholic faith; he is taking a great risk of social opprobrium. Yet across the United States, twenty-first-century seminaries are populated by young men who want to embrace the Gospel in full and who are uninterested in Catholic Lite.

Catholicism-in-full does not set "Gospel" against "doctrine". That is a Protestantizing move that has done grave damage to the Christian identity and witness of many Christian communities born from the Reformations of the sixteenth century. Catholicism-in-full recognizes that the basic Gospel proclamation—"Jesus is Lord"—was developed intellectually by a Spirit-led movement within the Church, which produced the Church's creeds and its defining dogmatic definitions. Catholicism-in-full also recognizes that, under the same divine inspiration, the Church's understanding of the truths that make the Church who she is develops over time—always in continuity with what has been handed on from the past. Thus Catholicism-in-full deploys both Gospel and doctrine in evangelization and pastoral ministry, believing that the full truth of Catholic faith is indeed liberating in the deepest meaning of human freedom.

The failures of Catholic Lite have been manifest for some time, and it takes a special kind arrogance, or just plain stubbornness, not to face the empirical facts of the contemporary Catholic situation. Catholic

Lite may have the capacity to maintain existing Catholic institutions for a time; Catholic Lite has demonstrated no capacity to grow those institutions or, more importantly, to transform them into platforms for evangelization and mission.

This suggests that, in the not-too-distant future, Catholic Lite will lead to "Catholic Zero", or something that looks alarmingly similar to Catholic Zero—a Catholicism that has lost any serious capacity for either mission or public witness. Examples of this can be found in both Europe and North America, in once-vibrant Catholic cultures and societies such as those in Québec, Spain, Portugal, and Ireland. These societies are now aptly described as "post-Christian". And in several cases, "post-Christian" is rapidly decaying into "anti-Christian", with the Church incapable of mounting any defense of the innocent against the culture of death, or of responding to the anti-Christian propaganda in politics, culture, and the media that seeks to drive the Church out of public life.

To repeat and sum up: there is no example, anywhere in the world, of Catholic Lite delivering on its promise of "relevance". Where Catholic Lite has infected local Churches, evangelical fervor has diminished and so has the Catholic capacity to shape humane societies. These situations are sometimes described, and by high-ranking churchmen, as a "pastoral emergency" for which more and lighter Catholic Lite is prescribed. The iron law of Christianity and modernity suggests an alternative diagnosis and prescription. The "emergency" is a collapse of deep faith that Jesus is Lord, which has led to a failure to proclaim the Gospel. The remedy is a vibrant Catholicism-in-full offering friendship with Jesus Christ and incorporation into the communion of his friends as the pathway to human happiness, fulfillment—and salvation.

The next pope must know these truths and lead the Church in light of them.

Caricatures to the contrary notwithstanding, Catholicism-in-full is not a revival of Jansenism or other forms of moral rigorism in the Church. The vibrant, living parts of the world Church are not those reserving the handclasp of fellowship to the already-perfected. The living parts of the world Church are those that offer friendship with Jesus Christ to those caught in the worship of false gods, be those the gods that terrify indigenous peoples or, in the West, the false god of the imperial autonomous Self—the false god "Me". The living parts of the world Church are those that offer mercy as well as truth, while recognizing that the most merciful thing a Christian can do for suffering or lost souls is to offer them the truth: that, in Jesus Christ, we meet the face of the merciful Father and the truth about ourselves—the Father who welcomes the prodigals home when they acknowledge that they have squandered their human dignity, and the truth that that dignity is magnified in Christ.

When a pope manifests the power of divine mercy in his own life, he empowers the people of the Church to be agents of that mercy in the world. The next pope must live and teach in such a way that the relationship between mercy and truth is clear, and he must live and teach in such a way that mercy (which the world often confuses with therapeutic forgetfulness) does not devolve into sentimentality. The divine mercy is purifying as well as comforting, and what can seem comforting will not be truly comforting over time if it is detached from purification.

Growth into the Christian life is a lifelong process for everyone, in a lesson that involves both truth and mercy. Catholics learn that lesson from the lives of the saints, beginning with Peter himself. The next pope must teach that lesson to a Church sometimes confused about the intimate relationship between mercy and truth, and should display the meaning of the lesson in his own self-emptying witness to Christ.

Over two millennia of Church history, preachers and teachers have arisen who claim to have found the long-forgotten or obscured key to the Gospel, and indeed to the entire edifice of Christian faith. Yet by placing inordinate emphasis on one or another truth of faith, these would-be reformers implicitly or explicitly degraded other truths of faith. In doing so, they deformed what they sought to lift up and failed to reform what needed reforming in the Church.

This temptation to reductionism—sometimes proclaimed in the name of an evangelical simplicity—unbalances the structure of faith and thereby does grave damage to the Church. It led to Church-dividing fractures in the first Christian millennium. Perhaps the most dramatic examples occurred during the Reformations of the sixteenth century, when what might have become the retrieval of certain important truths of faith resulted, not in the reforms sought, but in a severe breach in the Church's witness to the Gospel as the Christian world shattered, often violently.

Similar temptations occur in the contemporary Church. One, prominent in Latin America in the late twentieth century, was to find the lost key to the Gospel in the Lord's proclamation of justice for the poor. That reduction turned Catholic priests into political agents rather than evangelists and pastors. In the third decade of the twenty-first century, the divine mercy is often proclaimed as the forgotten key to the Gospel. This has led some to imagine that the divine mercy of which all stand in need can be set against the truths the Church teaches about what makes for righteous living and human happiness. The result is another exercise in Catholic Lite, in which a form of comfort is substituted for the true liberation of radical conversion to Christ and the Gospel.

When an essential truth of the Gospel becomes the only truth of the Gospel, the Gospel is distorted and its proclamation is impaired. The next pope must understand this and must teach the Church to resist the temptation to a simplification of the Gospel message that ends up in a distorted reduction of the Gospel message.

In order to preach and witness to the Gospel in full, and to help the world Church understand that the Gospel cannot be set against doctrine or mercy against truth, the next pope must recognize the great advances that have been made in Catholic moral theology in recent decades.

Catholic moral theology begins with the Beatitudes of Matthew 5:1–11: the Lord's description of what makes for human happiness. Thus legalism is foreign to a genuine Catholic understanding of the moral life. For some centuries the Church tended to forget this and Catholic moral theology was typically presented as a strict legal code. In the wake of Vatican II, certain attempts to reform moral theology exchanged a "hard" legalism for a "soft" legalism: the moral life was still about rules, but the rules were more elastic.

The deeper reform of Catholic moral theology since the Second Vatican Council has taught the living parts of the world Church to move beyond legalism, hard or soft, and to embrace a virtue-centered moral theology in which the goal of the moral life is goodness and beatitude. In this deeper reform, conversion to Christ is the beginning of the moral life. For it was Christ who came "that they may have life, and have it abundantly" (Jn 10:10), and it was

Christ who answered the young man's question about what "good" he must do to have eternal life (Mt 19:16).

Conversion to Christ then leads the Catholic to understand that God has provided guardrails for the journey to goodness and beatitude. Those guardrails are found in the moral law written on the human heart, in the moral law given to the people of Israel in Exodus 20:1–17, and in the Church's moral teaching, which is built on both revelation and reason. The "rules" of the moral life empower us to lead good lives, and ultimately lead us to beatitude; they are not arbitrary expressions of God's will, nor are they diktats of an authoritarian Church.

Viewed through the lens of conversion to Christ and understood in light of the Gospel, the moral life is not a matter of commands and duties alone, although it does involve commands and duties. In the light of the Gospel, the moral life is about goodness, happiness, and the virtues that make for goodness and happiness. Ultimately, the Christian moral life is about self-giving love—the kind of love that disposes of itself as gift, making us into the kind of people who can live for eternity in the light of the Holy Trinity, a communion of self-giving love and receptivity.

The next pope must understand this deep reform of Catholic moral theology and teach it to the Church, so that Catholics and those exploring Catholicism come to understand the moral life as a journey into virtue and toward beatitude.

The Great Commission of Matthew 28:19–20 commands the friends of the Lord Jesus to make disciples of all nations by teaching and baptizing. The Great Commission does not include instructions on dialogue or accompaniment. Dialogue and accompaniment can be useful tools in fulfilling the Great Commission. Dialogue and accompaniment can be helpful instruments in pastoral work, inviting the believer to grow more deeply into the liberating truths of the faith. Dialogue and accompaniment can help Christians to experience more fully the divine mercy. Dialogue and accompaniment are means only, however. They are not ends.

The proponents of Catholic Lite often seem to imagine that dialogue and accompaniment are all the Church can offer, and indeed all the Church should offer. This reduction of the Church's mission to dialogue and accompaniment may, in some minds, be the only possible Catholic response to increasingly secularized times. Yet that reduction is a great failure of Catholic imagination and purpose; it may be symptomatic of the collapse of supernatural and Christocentric faith, for which other forms of faith are then substituted. But neither a therapeutically oriented affirmation of Western narcissism nor an uncritical embrace of pagan religiosity nor a Gaia-centered eco-piety can substitute for the truth of God in Christ, revealed in the Gospel. The proclamation of that truth and that Gospel is what the Church is for.

The next pope must remind the entire Church of that.

The Next Pope, the Crisis
of the Human Person, and
Christian Humanism

*Grace was given to each of us according to the measure
of Christ's gift. . . . And his gifts were . . . for building
up the body of Christ, until we all attain to the unity
of the faith and of the knowledge of the Son of God,
to mature manhood, to the measure of the stature of
the fulness of Christ.*

—Ephesians 4:7, 11–13

***The next pope must understand that the
twenty-first-century crisis of world civilization
is a crisis in the idea of the human person
and that the answer to that crisis is the
revitalization of Christian humanism.***

Men of quite different personalities, theological sensibilities, intellectual and pastoral formations, and life experiences have held the Office of Peter in the twentieth and twenty-first centuries. It is striking, then, that amidst that diversity has run a common conviction: humanity's travails in the past century and a half have been rooted in defective understandings of the human person. It is not surprising that eleven different popes spoke of the nature and source of these defects in different keys. What is instructive is that those eleven Bishops of Rome agreed that the world crises through which they were leading the Church—which included two sanguinary world wars, a Cold War that threatened to destroy civilization, and a post–Cold War world failing to deliver on the hope for a new springtime of the human spirit—had something to do with a crisis in the great project of Western humanism.

The character of that crisis was neatly summed up by the French theologian Henri de Lubac, S.J., in a book published during World War II. There, the future theological *peritus* at Vatican II wrote that "it is not true, as is sometimes said, that man cannot organize the world without God. What is true is that, without God, he can only organize it against man."[1] Forty years after de Lubac, the Russian writer Aleksandr Solzhenitsyn made the same point even more succinctly: the disasters of the twentieth century, he proposed, had happened because men had forgotten God.

Absent the God of the Bible, it seems, humanism becomes self-destructive of both individuals and societies. Or as English historian Christopher Dawson, ordinarily the mildest of authors, put it in an uncharacteristically fierce passage, "a secular society that has no end beyond its own satisfaction is a monstrosity—a cancerous growth that will ultimately destroy itself."[2]

The popes of the twentieth and twenty-first centuries understood this, each in his own way. The next pope must understand it, too. And with the Church, he must propose Christian humanism—a humanism informed by the riches of biblical religion and centered on Christ—to an increasingly fragile and contentious world. In doing so, the next pope and the Church he leads will be retrieving and proclaiming the fundamental truth about the human person described by Saint Augustine in his *Confessions*: "Thou hast made us for thyself, O Lord, and our hearts are restless until they rest in Thee." Whenever and wherever that truth is recognized, the restlessness and fears of the modern heart are calmed, the hungers of the human heart satisfied, and the full measure of human dignity restored. That truth must, however, be proposed.

The Fathers of the Second Vatican Council responded to this global crisis in the idea of the human person in two passages in *Gaudium et Spes* (Joy and Hope), the Pastoral Constitution on the Church in the Modern World. Each of these passages informs the other, and the two should always be read in parallel.

In section 22 of *Gaudium et Spes*, the Council Fathers wrote that "it is only in the mystery of the Word made flesh that the mystery of man truly becomes clear. For ... Christ the Lord ... in the very revelation of the mystery of the Father and his love, fully reveals man to himself and brings to light his most high calling."[3] That "most high calling", the Council Fathers taught

in section 24 of *Gaudium et Spes*, is the human vocation to love: "man can fully discover his true self only
in a sincere giving of himself."[4]

Like the popes of the twentieth century whose
work preceded and made possible the Second Vatican Council, the Fathers of Vatican II found one
cancerous root of the modern world's crisis of crises
in a pseudo-religion of self-assertion. That idolatrous
worship of the Self did not only warp individual
lives. Like an aggressive sarcoma, it metastasized in
ideologies and political movements that could see in
"the other" only a someone or something to fear—a
someone or something that must be destroyed.

That was, of course, an old story, and some of the
earliest strata of the Bible preserved the memory of it
in the stories of Adam and Eve, and Cain and Abel.
In the modern world, however, that perennial human
temptation to self-sufficiency and self-assertion had
planetary consequences.

That is why the Second Vatican Council called for a
renewal of Christian humanism. That summons remains
valid for the next pope and the Church he leads.

To proclaim a Christ-centered humanism to the
twenty-first century and the third millennium
requires both conviction and nerve: the conviction
that Jesus Christ really does disclose the truth about
the human person in a unique and unsurpassable way,
and the nerve to make that proclamation in the face
of the various counterproposals on offer. The next

pope could help the Church humbly but confidently proclaim that true humanism is Christocentric if he helps the Church see more clearly the failures of those counterproposals.

Communism and socialism promised a world of economic and political equality, from which would come the withering away of the state and the liberation of the human person. Where, precisely, did that happen?

Various forms of consumerism promised satisfaction in the enjoyment of abundant material goods. Have those satisfactions, real as they may be, satisfied the deepest longings of the human heart?

The sexual revolution promised a human world of happiness with women and men liberated from old taboos and living as equals. Where, precisely, has that been true?

When the Church proclaims with Saint Paul that the measure of true human maturity is "the measure of the stature of the fulness of Christ" (Eph 4:13), it is proposing something far grander than the failed humanisms of the past several centuries.

It proclaims that the human person is not a random by-product of cosmic biochemical processes.

It proclaims that there is more to the human condition than the struggle for power, with power understood as someone's capacity to impose his will on someone (or everyone) else.

It proposes that the human person is not a twitching bundle of morally commensurable desires, the fulfillment of which is the meaning of "human rights" and an obligation of the state.

It proclaims that who we are is of far greater consequence than what we have; that living nobly is not for a select few alone; and that the gift of oneself to others in love is far more satisfying than the assertion of oneself against others.

The Catholic Church can proclaim all of this because it sees these truths about humanity manifest in Jesus Christ, crucified and risen.

The world of the twenty-first century, like the world of the twentieth, is threatened by diminished ideas of the human person, decadent ideas of human aspirations, and foreshortened notions of human destiny. So there is nothing for the next pope and the Church he leads to be ashamed of when the pope and the Church proclaim Jesus Christ as what he said he was: "the way, and the truth, and the life" (Jn 14:6). To be sure, there is much for which the Church should be ashamed, as it wrestles with its failures to live the truths it proclaims. But there is no shame in proposing that the dignity and value of the human person are fully revealed in Jesus Christ, who tells us the truth about who we are, why we have infinite value, and why our destiny is not oblivion. That is a far, far nobler concept of human nature and human possibility than anything else on offer in the twenty-first century.

The parts of the world Church that make that proclamation joyfully and unhesitatingly today are the living parts of the Catholic Church. The next pope must recognize that, and so must the Church he leads.

The Catholic proclamation of Christian humanism in the twenty-first century must include teaching the truth about freedom.

It's not news that the world is confused about the meaning of freedom. The world has been confused about freedom since the Garden of Eden, where, according to the biblical account in Genesis 3, the perennial human capacity to make a mess of things by thinking that freedom means I-did-it-my-way was first displayed. Contemporary misunderstandings of freedom reflect that ancient falsehood, primarily by identifying freedom with willfulness: a bad idea that has infected the humanistic project since William of Ockham injected it into the West's cultural bloodstream in the fourteenth century. Whenever someone uses "choice" as a conversation-ending trump card in contemporary debates about how we should live, an Ockhamite game is being played. And that game is part of the dumbing down, the diminishment, of the human person.

Every human being is born willful, as the parents of any two-year-old know. Human maturation involves transforming instinctive willfulness into virtuous choosing, which means choosing wisely. The mantra of "choice" to legitimate any desire is somewhat akin to a two-year-old banging on a piano, which is noise, not music. Choosing well—choosing what we can know to be good (because it makes for happiness) and doing so as a matter of habit—is like an accomplished pianist at the keyboard: disciplined learning transforms piano bangers into piano players, able to give pleasure to themselves and others, enriching their own humanity and that of others in the process. The moral guardrails the Church proposes aim to guide us into choosing wisely, which is typically a matter of lifetime learning.

Freedom detached from goodness and reduced to "choice" is infantile. It does not make for happiness or satisfaction. It is also bad for society. For if there is only "your choice" and "my choice" and our choices collide, what happens when neither of us acknowledges that there is something called "the good" by which we can decide which of our choices is better (for the chooser and for society as a whole)? What happens is that one of us imposes our power on the other, or gets the state to do so. And that is a prescription for tyranny.

Just as it offers a nobler vision of human nature and human destiny by proclaiming Jesus Christ as the embodiment of a true humanism, the Catholic Church has a nobler idea of freedom to teach. The next pope must know that, must teach it, and must empower the Church he leads to live it and teach it.

The development of a rich philosophical and theological vision of the human person—a rich Christian anthropology—has been one of the signal accomplishments of Catholic intellectual life in the post-Vatican II era. That anthropology has underwritten some creative developments in Catholic moral theology, not least in the various John Paul II Institutes that were established throughout the world to draw Catholic moral theology beyond the old, tired debates between hard legalism and soft legalism and into a new approach to the moral life: an approach focused on goodness and beatitude. The next pope must appreciate these achievements and lift them up before the entire world Church, for they demonstrate that the Catholic Church offers a compelling, compassionate, and uplifting "picture" of the human person, which is essential for evangelization. In doing so, the next pope will also help Catholic thinkers resist the temptation to accommodate to the academic fashions of the day, especially in the fields of "gender studies", "queer studies", and other idolatries of the Self.

The Next Pope and the Bishops

*Jesus said to them again, "Peace be with you. As the
Father has sent me, even so I send you." And when
he had said this, he breathed on them, and said to
them, "Receive the Holy Spirit."*

—John 20:21–22

**The next pope must strengthen the episcopate and
reform the process by which bishops are selected.**

The First Vatican Council was interrupted in 1870
by the Franco-Prussian War, which broke out shortly
after the Council defined the circumstances under
which the Bishop of Rome could teach infallibly on
matters of faith and morals. Once peace was restored,
it was thought, the Council might reconvene; but
Vatican I was never called back into session. So what
had first been thought an interruption or adjournment
became a permanent suspension. Vatican I remained
in that limbo-like state until July 14, 1960, when Pope
John XXIII announced that the impending ecumenical council would be known as Vatican II.

Because of this accident of history, the Fathers of
Vatican I never had a chance to complete their work

on the locus and exercise of authority in the Church with a reflection on the authority of the Church's bishops. Vatican I's theology of the Church was thus somewhat truncated. The result was a certain imbalance in the Catholic imagination about the higher ranks of the Church's ordained leadership, with the papacy playing such a dominant role as to diminish the responsibilities of bishops. In some Catholic minds, local bishops were the branch managers of a vast global corporation whose primary function was to execute what the Chief Executive Officer in Rome decreed.

The Second Vatican Council sought to rebalance the Church's understanding of its leadership by carefully considering the office of bishop in itself, and by thinking through the relationship of the bishops to each other and to the Bishop of Rome. These questions led to considerable debate at Vatican II. Eventually, though, the Council Fathers agreed by overwhelming majorities on several key points.

In *Lumen Gentium*, the Dogmatic Constitution on the Church, the Council taught that the episcopate exists by the will of Christ; that the episcopate is the highest grade of the Sacrament of Holy Orders; that the exercise of the episcopal authority conferred by ordination is dependent on a bishop's communion with the Bishop of Rome; that those who receive episcopal ordination form a college that exercises full authority in the Church and shares responsibility for the Church's mission; and that this college always and only functions with and under the Bishop of Rome.

The Council's theology of the episcopate and its teaching on the relationship of the bishops to the universal pastor of the Church implicitly rejected the "CEO/branch-manager" model of the-pope-and-the-bishops (which had never been a matter of doctrine). Having received the fullness of Holy Orders by his episcopal ordination, the local bishop, according to Vatican II, is a vicar of Christ in his local Church. He can only exercise that leadership with and under the Bishop of Rome. But he is a true vicar of Christ, not just a vicar of the pope.

The CEO/branch-manager model was also quietly buried by the Council's teaching on episcopal collegiality. Vatican I taught authoritatively that the unique authority of the Bishop of Rome extends to the entire Church and could be exercised directly; this was a critically important affirmation of the Church's independence at a historical moment when modern states were seeking in various ways to exercise control over local bishops and local Churches. Vatican II complemented this teaching on the pope's universal jurisdiction by affirming that the bishops as a body—a college—share responsibility for the universal Church, such that a local bishop's responsibilities do not end at the borders of his diocese. As a member of the episcopal college, his relationship with his brother bishops involves a responsibility to come to their aid when necessary, to consult with them on matters of common concern, and to offer fraternal correction when required. And as the Bishop of Rome is a member of the College of

Bishops as well as its head, his brother bishops have a responsibility to help him, consult with him, and, if necessary, correct him, as he does with them.

In teaching these things, the Second Vatican Council was engaging in authentic Catholic reform, which always involves the recovery of some aspect of the Church's Christ-given "form" that has languished or been forgotten. In this case, the reform meant retrieving and renewing the relationship that existed among the Church's bishops, and between the bishops and the Bishop of Rome, during the mid-first millennium—the era of the great Fathers of the Church and the first ecumenical councils, when Catholicism was formulating crucial doctrinal definitions and taking its definitive shape as a hierarchically ordered community. Vatican II did not, however, describe precisely how this complex relationship of mutual episcopal responsibility for the Church under an authoritative head was to function. The debate about that "how" remains serious and intense, more than a half-century after the Council's conclusion. As has been the case throughout the history of the Church, it will likely take a considerable amount of time to discern how post-Vatican II structures like national conferences of bishops and the world Synod of Bishops best function for the sake of the proclamation of the Gospel.

What should be obvious now, though, is that competent management does not exhaust the proper exercise of the office of bishop in a local

Church. Competent management is essential, but it cannot be understood as the deepest meaning of the office of bishop. Moreover, the fullness of Holy Orders that is conferred with episcopal ordination is not akin to a military officer's promotion to the highest rank in his or her branch of service. There is far more to the episcopate than rank, just as there is far more to the papacy than rank.

As the head of a local Church who bears the fullness of Holy Orders, the bishop is the chief teacher of the faith in the diocese given to his care—which is to say, he is the local Church's chief witness to the Gospel and its principal evangelist.

Lumen Gentium clearly taught that evangelism is the bishop's primary responsibility: because the Gospel the apostles were commanded to teach "is, for the Church, the principle of all its life for all time", the successors of the apostles—the bishops—"receive from the Lord ... the mission of teaching all peoples, and of preaching the Gospel to every creature, so that all men may attain to salvation by faith, baptism and the observance of the commandments.... [Thus] among the more important duties of bishops that of preaching the Gospel has pride of place."[1] Such a responsibility cannot be delegated, although it can and must be shared with a local Church's clergy and people. The local bishop will not, however, empower his priests and people to be missionary disciples unless he is first an evangelist himself.

As the bishop of a local Church, the bishop is the chief sanctifier of his diocese, a role he exercises through the celebration of the sacraments. The bishop shares this responsibility with the priests of his local Church. Further, the bishop's sanctification of his people will empower all those under his pastoral care to exercise the priestly role conferred on them at baptism, when they were consecrated by the Holy Spirit to offer true worship to the Thrice-Holy God. The bishop will do this best, for both his priests and his people, when he manifests the grace and power of the sacraments at work in his own life.

And, as the head of a local Church exercising the fullness of Holy Orders, the bishop is the chief governor of his diocese. In the West, this has often come to mean that the local bishop spends the greater part of his time in managing ecclesiastical affairs (including the diocesan finances) and negotiating the rocks and shoals of the local Church's relationship to society and the state. Many bishops chafe under this, which is nothing new; Saint Gregory the Great complained about the burdens of administration in a late sixth-century homily that the Church reads on his liturgical memorial. In the mind of Vatican II, though (as in the mind of Gregory the Great), the priority tasks of the bishop are evangelizing, teaching, and sanctifying. The most effective local bishops in the twenty-first-century Church are those who have learned to do the works of governance and management in cooperation with competent clergy and laity, so that they have as much time as possible for the work of evangelism and for the celebration of the sacraments with their people.

In the Latin-Rite Catholic Church, it falls to the
Bishop of Rome to appoint men who can fulfill these
episcopal responsibilities, as it falls to the Bishop of
Rome to confirm the choice of men for the office
of bishop proposed by the synods of the Eastern Catholic Churches. How does the Church of the twenty-
first century—a Church in mission—know who these
men are?

The Church knows these men because they have
already demonstrated the capacity to be evangelists,
sanctifiers, and governors. In both West and East,
the process of discerning such men is enhanced by
consultation with those who know a potential can-
didate for the episcopate and can judge his capabilities to lead in apostolic times. The next pope must
recognize this and insist that such consultations—
emphasizing the assessment of a man's capacities to
be a herald of the Gospel—be undertaken before
candidates for the episcopate are presented to him.

Popes do many things, but there are only two things
a pope must do. He must appoint bishops or confirm their election by the synods of the Eastern Catholic Churches, because he alone has the authority to
do so. And he must receive the ambassadors of states
with whom the Holy See has full diplomatic relations,
because he is bound by treaty to do so. Of these two
tasks, the appointment of bishops is more important
by orders of magnitude. The next pope must recognize that. And the next pope must refine the process

by which the Church selects bishops so that the bishops of the twenty-first century meet the requirements of episcopal ministry in apostolic times that call for a vigorous proclamation of the Gospel.

In the third decade of the twenty-first century, there are some thirty-two hundred local jurisdictions in the Catholic Church, involving a vast diversity of cultural, social, political, economic, and religious situations. The next pope must find bishops who can reevangelize post-Christian (and often aggressively anti-Christian) societies, and he must find bishops who can evangelize pagan societies that have never heard the Gospel. The next pope must find bishops who can ignite evangelical fervor in wealthy local Churches, and he must find bishops who can build local Churches from the bottom up with limited financial resources. The next pope must also find bishops who can defend their people against persecutors of various sorts, bishops willing to lay down their lives if necessary for the sake of the flock entrusted to their care. Is there any template adequate to identifying men capable of being bishops in such various circumstances?

There is. The next pope should know it and implement it.

The qualities required of twenty-first-century bishops throughout the world Church are not a mystery—if it is understood that, wherever the Church is, the Church is in mission.

Bishops of a Church in mission must be radically converted disciples who have demonstrated in their lives a personal conversion to Jesus Christ and a conscious choice to abandon everything to follow the Lord Jesus.

Bishops of a Church in mission must have shown evangelical energy and capacity, boldly and effectively proclaiming the Gospel and thus bringing others into the Catholic communion of disciples in mission. This evangelical energy must include the ability to make the Christian proposal to nonbelievers, to rekindle the flame of faith in Catholics who have drifted away from the Church, and the willingness to admonish and correct Catholics who have embraced ideas and practices contrary to the Gospel. These qualities will be evident in the growth of the parishes a man has served or the vitality of the campus ministries, other forms of chaplaincy, or seminaries he has served or led.

Bishops of a Church in mission must have demonstrated a capacity to sanctify the people of the Church by leading them into a deeper experience of the paschal mystery of Jesus Christ, crucified and risen, in the sacred liturgy.

Bishops of a Church in mission must have the courage to be countercultural, which means the courage to challenge deformed cultural norms in the name of the Gospel and the truths it teaches about the human person.

Bishops of a Church in mission must have the courage to make decisions that will be unpopular, if such decisions are necessary to maintain or restore discipline in the Church and to defend authentic Catholic teaching. This means, among other things, finding men who will not pass their legitimate local responsibilities to "Rome", in the hope that "Rome will take care of it."

Above all, the bishop of a Church in mission must be able to call others to holiness of life because he manifests Christian holiness, the joy of the Gospel, and the workings of divine mercy in his own life.

There are two dicasteries in the Roman Curia that help the pope in the selection of bishops. The next pope, knowing that the qualities just cited are required of bishops in a twenty-first-century Church in mission, must select leaders for those dicasteries who share that understanding and who will, with the next pope, reform the process of selecting bishops accordingly.

That reform must include broadening the consultations that lead to a man's nomination for the episcopate. As the nomination process operates today, it often happens that those consulted are primarily, even only, bishops. This is a mistake that has led to grave problems for the Church, and the next pope should rectify it.

Bishops-naming-bishops amplifies the temptation for the episcopate to think of itself, to act, and to reproduce itself as a higher form of clerical caste. It tends to marginalize good candidates for the episcopate who may make less-competent or less evangelically fervent men, themselves already bishops, nervous or uncomfortable. It can reinforce the worst aspects of clericalism, with priests jockeying for the favor of their own bishop or other bishops. And it tends to eliminate from the nomination process those who may know a man's strengths (and weaknesses) better than his brother priests or his bishop: the people he has served in a parish, chaplaincy, or seminary. In too many situations that have come to light in the twenty-first century, grief and scandal could have been prevented had competent, shrewd lay people been asked confidentially about this or that potential nominee for the episcopate.

Ways to consult the laity in the nomination of bishops must therefore be devised. That does not mean conducting elections on the Anglican or Lutheran models. It does mean that the next pope should instruct the papal representatives through whom such nominations flow to the Vatican to garner suggestions for episcopal candidates from knowledgeable and faithful lay Catholics before nominations are sent to Rome. Lay Catholics should also be consulted on the names suggested by priests and bishops.

The pope's traditional *sollicitudo omnium ecclesiarum* (care for all the Churches) includes papal care for the Church's bishops, who are the pope's fellow workers in a college whose members bear responsibility for both their local Churches and the universal Church. This complex relationship requires the Bishop of Rome to be both brother and father.

The brotherhood of the pope and the bishops can be strengthened by papal meetings with a local episcopate when the Bishop of Rome is on pilgrimage in a given country. It should also be strengthened by the ancient tradition of the *ad limina* visit, by which all bishops fulfill their obligation to come every five years to "the threshold of the apostles", praying at the tombs of Saint Peter and Saint Paul; those pilgrimages are also occasions for meeting with the Successor of Peter and his collaborators. In the post-Vatican II era, *ad limina* visits have worked best when they are opportunities for genuine conversation between local bishops, on the one hand, and the pope and his collaborators, on the other. The next pope can make this tradition more vital in empowering the bishops for evangelization and sanctification by ensuring that his own conversations with the bishops and their discussions with curial officials focus on the challenges of being a Church in mission, and by the pope celebrating the Eucharist with bishops on their *ad limina* visits.

The fatherhood of the pope in relationship to the bishops must include the disciplining and, if necessary, removal of bishops, when that is necessary for the credibility of the Gospel and the spiritual health of a local Church.

The next pope must be willing to remove from office bishops whose personal behavior has become a countersign to the Gospel. The next pope must be willing to remove from office bishops who teach a doctrine other than that of the Catholic Church. The next pope must be willing to remove bishops whose manifest incompetence in governance has irretrievably damaged their capacity to lead.

Thus the next pope must recognize that far greater damage is done to the cause of the Gospel, to the morale of the Church's people, and to the Church's public credibility by leaving a corrupt, malfeasant, or incompetent bishop in office than by removing him. More damage is also done to that man's soul.

The strengthening and reform of the episcopate in the Catholic Church of the twenty-first century, so that the Church might be ever more vigorously a Church in mission, must be complemented by strengthening the College of Cardinals.

As the popes of the mid-twentieth century insisted on reforming the episcopate by ordaining native-born bishops in missionary lands (often against the opposition of colonial powers), the popes of the late twentieth and early twenty-first centuries have worked to strengthen the College of Cardinals by internationalizing it. On occasion, popes have also used the College as a kind of senate of papal consultors; such a consultation eventually led to the promulgation of the encyclical *Evangelium Vitae* in 1995.[2]

Because the College of Cardinals is responsible for the election of the Bishop of Rome, the next pope should ensure that the cardinal-electors—the members of the College who have not yet reached their eightieth birthday—have a knowledge of the world

Church and a familiarity with the challenges to evangelization that occur in different local situations. Broadening the papal electorate nationally or geographically ought not result in a diminishment of the College's capabilities and capacities. The next pope should work to develop those capabilities and capacities, and not only by his appointments.

Thus the next pope, in addition to choosing cardinals with significant knowledge or experience of the Church's situation beyond their immediate locales, should see to it that the College of Cardinals meets with some regularity. This practice has fallen into abeyance and it ought to be restored, not least because it is necessary in preparing conclaves for the election of a pope. A College of Cardinals in which the members really do not know one another cannot function well as an electoral body. Only if the members of the College already have some knowledge of each other, so that they can speak to each other freely and with mutual confidence, will they be able to work well together when they undertake the difficult task of choosing the Successor of Peter, the Bishop of Rome.

The Next Pope and the Church's Priests

"For behold, the kingdom of God is in your midst."

—Luke 17:21

***The next pope must intensify the reform of
the priesthood and the consecrated life.***

The Gospel challenges believers in every time and
place to recognize that the promised transformation
of all things, which the New Testament calls the
"kingdom of God", has begun among us. The Kingdom is present in the person of the Risen Lord Jesus
in the communion of the Church, Christ's Mystical
Body in the world. The Kingdom is present where
the Beatitudes are lived and the power of God is made
visible in those whom the world deems of little or
no account. Through the grace of the sacraments, the
radically converted disciple lives the life of the Kingdom every day and offers those who have not yet met
the Lord Jesus the possibility of a share in his life.

Christians thus live in a unique time zone, a Kingdom time zone. For what Christians believe will be
manifest in glory at the end of history—the fulfillment

of Christ's promise to "make all things new" (Rev 21:5)—is in fact unfolding now, in history. So when the Church follows the Lord's instruction and prays several times each day "thy kingdom come", the Church is praying for the fuller manifestation of a reality that Jesus proclaimed to be breaking into history in his own person and mission. That proclamation was vindicated by the Resurrection, in which the truth about human destiny was revealed in such a powerful way that the friends of the Risen One went out and began the conversion of the world by the preaching of the Gospel.

Over two millennia of Christian history, different vocations in the Church have developed to make this Kingdom dimension of the Church's life visible in a heightened way, and to give concrete expression to the Lord's assurance that the reign of God is not just "future", but is also "present". Such vocations manifest an individual's desire to be entirely possessed by God. Those vocations also have an important ecclesial function, for their radical witness to the "present" of the Kingdom of God among us serves to call the entire Church to a more complete configuration to Christ and to a more vigorous proclamation of the Gospel.

These radically Kingdom-centered vocations include the priesthood of the New Covenant and the vowed religious life consecrated by the evangelical counsels or counsels of perfection (poverty, chastity, and obedience). The priesthood and the consecrated life function as a kind of spiritual reactor core in the

Church, from which radiates the energy that empowers evangelization and mission throughout the entire communion of disciples. The health of the priesthood and the consecrated life at any moment in history are thus indices of the vitality of the Church of that time, for it is through the priesthood and the consecrated life that the Church experiences in a more radical way the truth that the Kingdom of God is among us.

The reform of the priesthood and the consecrated life is an essential component of the New Evangelization. The next pope must therefore see to the intensification of that reform, which has been underway for decades in the face of many obstacles and setbacks.

In the third decade of the twenty-first century, there are some four hundred thousand ordained priests in the Catholic Church. Many of them are men of outstanding virtue. More than a few of them do the work of evangelization and sanctification in situations of staggering difficulty. Despite these examples of goodness, however, the "story" of the Catholic priesthood as the world reads it is often a story of crisis. And there are elements of truth in that story, however distorted its overall portrayal of twenty-first-century Catholic life may be.

More Catholic priests left the active ministry in the years immediately following the Second Vatican Council than at any time since the Reformations of the sixteenth century. Then, as a reform of priestly formation and priestly service was beginning to show real, evangelical effects at the beginning of the twenty-first century, the world Church was rocked by revelations of sexual abuse by priests dating back decades. Sexual abuse of the young is a plague throughout the world; the tawdry record of clerical sexual abuse was especially devastating in a Church in which the ordained priesthood had long been held in high esteem.

The crisis of the priesthood is global in character. And while that crisis takes distinctive forms in different cultures and societies, the twenty-first-century crisis of the Catholic priesthood, in every context, is fundamentally a crisis of fidelity and identity. Priests who truly believe what the Catholic Church teaches about the nature of the ordained priesthood—that it is a unique participation in the one, eternal priesthood of Jesus Christ—are not sexual abusers; nor do they betray their promise of perpetual chastity in other ways. Priests who understand that their ministry is far more than a set of functions—that it is a vocation that manifests in a distinctive way the presence of the Kingdom of God among us—do not abuse the respect given them by the people of the Church by acting autocratically, or worse.

The next pope must grasp that the crisis of the priesthood in the twenty-first century is a crisis of fidelity and identity. Only then can he call the Church's priests to a deeper understanding and more radical living of the unique character that Christ bestows on the priests of the New Covenant. The next pope must remind the entire Church that priestly ordination does not only empower a man to perform certain sacramental acts; priestly ordination transforms a man into an icon of the "great high priest ... Jesus, the Son of God" (Heb 4:14). In reminding the Church of that essential truth of Catholic faith, the next pope will remind the Church's priests of what took place in them on the day of their ordinations.

These reminders are essential in combating the evils of clericalism, which traduces the priesthood of the New Covenant by imagining the priest as a member of a caste—a temptation to which both priests and people are subject. While that caste consciousness does not cause abusive behavior, sexual or otherwise, it can facilitate clerical sexual abuse and the clerical abuse of authority. Thus the next pope must constantly remind both priests and people that the Catholic priesthood is not a caste but an order: a unique configuration of men to Christ. That unique configuration constitutes the ordained as a brotherhood; it does not, and must not be allowed to, create a caste.

The next pope must also encourage the Church's priests, thank them for their sacrifice, and inspire his brothers in the priesthood to live in a way commensurate with the dignity of their vocation. He will best do this by manifesting in his own life the joy of the priesthood and its distinctive form of self-giving love. That vocation to radical, self-sacrificial love is challenging under any circumstances; it is particularly challenging in cultures deeply wounded by the sexual revolution. The priesthood of the New Covenant in the Catholic Church calls a man to exercise paternal love in a unique and countercultural way. Priests deserve the support of their bishop, their brother priests, and their people in meeting that challenge to spiritual fatherhood. They also deserve the support, gratitude, and encouragement of the Bishop of Rome.

One way the next pope can offer that encouragement and support is by affirming the gift that priestly celibacy is to the Church. And the next pope should explain the nature of that gift to the entire Church so that the Church can explain it to the world. It is sometimes said, even by senior churchmen, that celibacy makes no sense in certain cultural situations. That is, of course, true, if the cultural situation in question is pagan or post-Christian. The sacrifice involved in celibate love and the gift that such self-sacrifice offers to God and to the Church only make sense in the context of the Kingdom present among us. And if the Gospel of the Kingdom has not been proclaimed, whether in the rain forests of Brazil or the cities of Germany, the celibate form of paternal love will make little or no sense.

By the same token, however, the radical self-gift embodied in the celibate priesthood can, in the context of preaching the Gospel and proclaiming the Kingdom, be a powerful witness to the presence of Christ among us. Thus the next pope will take care to teach the Church that the celibate love of the Latin-Rite priesthood is a manifestation of the Kingdom among us here and now, and a unique participation in the total self-giving displayed by Jesus Christ, whose life, death, and Resurrection inaugurated the priesthood of the New Covenant.

In doing this, the next pope will remind the Church and teach the world that the self-sacrificing love of celibacy is a sign that the priesthood of the New Covenant is a matter of what a man *is* before it is a question of what a man *does*. Ordained priesthood in the Catholic Church is not priestcraft; ordained priesthood in the Catholic Church is iconography, a making-present of the priesthood of Jesus Christ through the person of the ordained priest. The celibate Catholic priest is not a bachelor; the Catholic priest is a spiritual father who has been configured by Holy Orders to Christ the Good Shepherd. The living parts of the Catholic Church understand this; the dying or moribund parts of the Catholic Church typically think in terms of priestcraft rather than priesthood. Correcting that misconception of the priesthood of the New Covenant is essential to recovering the fullness of Catholic faith in the lands of Catholic Lite, where the desacralization of the priesthood is one crucial factor in the collapse of Catholic faith and practice.

The next pope must call the priests of the Church to be men of God who teach others how to worship the living God by leading them in godly worship.

The Second Vatican Council, in *Lumen Gentium*, taught the Church that the sacred liturgy is the "source and summit" of the Church's life, from which all else flows.[1] The Church's liturgy is—or should be—another mission-empowering experience of the unique Christian time zone that is the life of the Kingdom here and now. Thus the Council Fathers wrote in *Sacrosanctum Concilium*:

> In the earthly liturgy we take part in a foretaste of the heavenly liturgy which is celebrated in the Holy City of Jerusalem toward which we journey as pilgrims, where Christ is sitting at the right hand of God, minister of the holies and of the true tabernacle. With all the warriors of the heavenly army we sing a hymn of glory to the Lord; venerating the memory of the saints, we hope for some part and fellowship with them; we eagerly await the Saviour, Our Lord Jesus Christ, until he our life shall appear and we too will appear with him in glory.[2]

The Bishop of Rome is not, of course, the liturgical director of every parish in the Catholic world. His own celebration of the liturgy is now on display to the entire Church, however, because of the communications revolution that has reshaped the world's experience of the papacy. Thus in his liturgical ministry in Rome, and when he celebrates the liturgy among the People of God when he is on pilgrimage to local Churches, the next pope's priestly service should be transparent to the priesthood of Jesus Christ. That transparency will help his priests realize in their own lives the truth of what they have been ordained to be, even as it empowers the members of the Church to exercise the privilege of offering right worship that was conferred on them by the gift of the Holy Spirit in baptism.

Human beings are theotropic: they will worship something. Understanding this, the next pope will do everything in his power to see that the Church, through the liturgical ministry of its priests, displays before the world the beauty, dignity, and power of right worship.

"Vocation recruitment"—proposing that men consider the ordained priesthood as a demanding yet fulfilling way to live their Christian commitment—is most effective when Catholic leaders, including the pope, lift up a heroic vision of the priesthood and challenge men to live the drama of radical self-sacrifice. Thus the next pope should insist that the reform of the Church's seminaries— which is well advanced in some parts of the world Church but has barely begun in others—must inculcate in future priests an understanding of the sacredness of the priestly vocation. That understanding begins with radical conversion to the Gospel. It then expresses itself in a special configuration to Christ the Lord that is lived in paternal self-sacrifice, not in a clerical caste system.

No seminary system has ever been perfect or ever will be. Seminaries that stress the imperative of radical conversion and priestly self-sacrifice are, however, more likely to succeed in forming pastors after the heart of Christ. They are also more likely to weed out those who, for a variety of spiritual and psychological reasons, are incapable of living a priesthood of strong paternal love.

The next pope would also do well to encourage seminaries to lay more stress than most do now on the art of preaching. Unlike those Protestant ministers who think of themselves primarily as teachers (and thus work hard to develop themselves as preachers), Catholic priests tend to think of themselves primarily as celebrants of the sacraments. The Catholic Church of the New Evangelization needs pastors who are compelling preachers as well as sacramental sanctifiers whose celebration of the liturgy invites people into an experience of the paschal mystery. The Church of the New Evangelization needs priests who, while celebrating Mass, empower their people through their preaching to see the world afresh through biblical lenses.

The next pope should recognize that many of the reforms of the priesthood essential for a Church in mission apply in a direct or analogous way to the reform of the consecrated religious life.

Throughout the history of the Church, the Holy Spirit has raised up great reformers of religious communities of men and women, such as Saint John of the Cross and Saint Teresa of Ávila. The reformers' insistence that their communities return to a strict observance of the evangelical counsels typically met with considerable resistance, as similar reformers do today. It is all the more important, then, for the next pope to encourage, and indeed insist upon, a deep-reaching reform of consecrated religious life throughout the Church.

In the last decades of the twentieth century and the first decades of the twenty-first, too many religious communities became impediments to the proclamation of the Gospel in the New Evangelization because they tolerated patterns of behavior—especially in living the virtue of chastity—that were countersigns to the truths of the Gospel and of Catholic faith. Toleration of unchastity in religious communities is typically accompanied by dissent from authoritative Church teaching. And the latter is used to justify the former in a vicious circle of infidelity.

The Second Vatican Council, in *Perfectae Caritatis*, called all religious communities of consecrated life to recover their original "charism" or inspiration, and to make that recovery the basis of an authentically Catholic reform of their way of life and their mission. Too often, however, there was little or no recovery and too much accommodation to prevailing cultural mores. In the West, that accommodation led to the collapse of many venerable men's and women's communities of consecrated life. Others became enclaves of doctrinal and behavioral dissent from the truths of the Gospel. Conversely, those communities that rejected the path of cultural accommodation and that renewed themselves through an intensified commitment to the evangelical counsels showed an impressive capacity to grow, not merely survive, under extremely challenging social and cultural circumstances—and to become important contributors to the Church's work of evangelization and service.

The next pope must recognize the truths behind these contrasting patterns of renewal and collapse and their relationship to Gospel fidelity and infidelity. The next pope must also encourage—and protect—those authentic reformers who are working to renew their communities according to their unique inspiration, always in conformity with the Gospel and the truths authoritatively taught by the Church. And if necessary in exceptional cases, the next pope must himself take action in the life of religious communities that have shown themselves resistant to the reforms necessary to restore their capacity to be heralds of the Gospel and witnesses to the Kingdom present among us now.

The Next Pope and the Lay Apostolate

"You are the light of the world. A city set on a hill cannot be hidden. Nor do men light a lamp and put it under a bushel, but on a stand, and it gives light to all in the house. Let your light so shine before men, that they may see your good works and give glory to your Father who is in heaven."

—Matthew 5:14–16

The new pope must remind lay Catholics that they are the New Israel, the beloved people of the New Covenant, called to missionary discipleship now and to the Wedding Feast of the Lamb for eternity.

The Spirit-led journey on which the Catholic Church has been embarked since the pontificate of Pope Leo XIII has enriched the Church's self-understanding in many ways. Among the most significant of these developments was the development of a rich theology of the laity, a topic of little theological interest during the centuries when Counter-Reformation ecclesiology dominated the Church's thinking about itself. In that Counter-Reformation Church it was sometimes said that lay Catholics had three functions: to "pray, pay, and obey". (A contemporary of Saint John Henry Newman, Monsignor George Talbot, once offered an upper-class English variant on this theme: the laity were "to hunt, to shoot, to entertain".) Counter-Reformation Catholicism understood "the Church" in strictly hierarchical terms; lay Catholics were located firmly at the bottom of a pyramid in which both authority and initiative flowed in one direction, from the top to the bottom.

There were exceptions to this, which would prove fruitful in the Gospel-centered development of Catholic self-understanding that has led the Church into the New Evangelization.

Alert students of missiology knew, for example, that Catholicism on the Korean peninsula was originally an indigenous lay movement where the work of evangelization was carried out by lay leaders until a French missionary bishop was sent to Korea in 1836 (at the urging of lay Catholics). In Europe, which remained the Church's heartland well into the twentieth century, various lay movements of "Catholic Action" developed in response to the challenges of cultural, social, and political modernity. These movements were, in the main, firmly under hierarchical control. But the fact of their existence and their prominence in many countries prompted more serious theological reflection on the religious responsibilities of all the baptized—and on the possibilities of lay participation, even leadership, in the work of evangelization. Pope

Pius XII's 1943 encyclical *Mystici Corporis Christi* (The Mystical Body of Christ) nudged the Church beyond its accustomed pyramidal and juridical self-concept. Throughout the mid-twentieth century, lay scholars of international renown such as Jacques Maritain and Etienne Gilson made important contributions to the renewal of Catholic intellectual life. In 1953, the French Dominican theologian Yves Congar published *Jalons pour une théologie du laicat* (*Lay People in the Church*), an exploratory reflection that helped prepare the intellectual ground for the Second Vatican Council. Creative theological work on this theme was also done by the Swiss theologian Hans Urs von Balthasar, who described distinctive "lay" styles of theological reflection in the third volume of *The Glory of the Lord: A Theological Aesthetics*.

These developments came to a first moment of maturation when the Fathers of Vatican II devoted the fifth chapter of the Dogmatic Constitution on the Church to the "call to holiness" and its universality. The concept may have been unfamiliar to some, but this was no innovation; Saint Paul himself had spoken of his first Christian communities as "the saints" (e.g., see Eph 1:1). So in reminding all Catholics that they had been consecrated to holiness in Baptism, the Council Fathers were, once again, calling the Church back to its Gospel origins in order to find inspiration and evangelical energy for the third millennium of Christian history.

Vatican II's teaching on the universal call to holiness also implied a certain de-clericalization of the

Church. The Church was and would remain hier-archically ordered by the will of Christ, and govern-ing authority in the Church would always be linked to the Sacrament of Holy Orders. Yet the Council insisted that sanctity—that graced quality that the Church exists to foster—was not for the church sanc-tuary alone. Sanctity is every Christian's vocation, in the world as well as when in church. That vocation is conferred at the beginning of Christian life, in the Sacrament of Baptism.

In the days when the Catholic Church in the West fit comfortably within the local culture, baptism was often understood as an institutional initiation rite: a sacrament, to be sure, but also a tribal or ethnic wel-coming ritual. The Council's theology of the universal call to holiness called all Catholics to appropriate the meaning of their baptism in full: to be baptized is to be configured to Jesus Christ, the incarnate Son of God, and thus to become a member of his Mystical Body, the Church that continues Christ's work in the world.

To be baptized, then, is to share in the three offices of Christ as priest, prophet, and king. To be bap-tized empowers a Catholic to offer right worship to the one true God (the priestly office). To be baptized is to be consecrated to speak and bear witness to the truth for the conversion of the world (the prophetic office). And to be baptized is to share in Christ's servant-kingship by living the Beatitudes for the heal-ing of the world's brokenness.

And according to the Council's theology of the laity as authoritatively interpreted and developed by Pope John Paul II in the 1988 apostolic exhortation *Christifideles Laici* (Christ's Faithful Lay People) and the 1991 encyclical *Redemptoris Missio* (The Mission of the Redeemer), to be baptized is to be given the Great Commission—the mandate to offer friendship with the Lord Jesus to "all nations". On this understanding of the Council's teaching, every Catholic is a missionary. For to be baptized is to be a disciple, and the mission to offer others the gift one has been given—the gift of friendship with the Lord Jesus—is an implicit responsibility of discipleship. The Great Jubilee of 2000 was intended to remind the world Church of these truths of baptism, and the Jubilee-closing apostolic letter, *Novo Millennio Ineunte*, emphasized the missionary responsibility of the entire Church to "put out into the deep" of evangelism.

The centrality of the universal call to holiness in Vatican II's teaching on the nature of the Church, and the teaching of both the Council and the post-conciliar popes on lay responsibility for witness and evangelization, have been insufficiently understood by Catholic laity and clergy alike. That lack of understanding has resulted in confusions and distortions. So the next pope must lift up the universal call to holiness and the universal responsibility to evangelize as rooted in the baptismal character conferred on every Christian. And he must lead in such a way that these truths are worked more thoroughly into the texture of Catholic life in all its expressions.

Clericalism means many things, including a warped sense of power among clergymen who manifest a destructive misconception of sacerdotal authority. In its broader sense, however, "clericalism" is the notion, explicitly stated or tacitly assumed, that only the clergy "count" in the Church. This notion is found across the spectrum of Catholic opinion; it is false: and it too often results in a clericalized laity and a laicized clergy—lay people who imagine that holding some office or exercising some form of executive responsibility in the Church is the real meaning of discipleship, and clergy who think of Holy Orders as merely a license to conduct certain forms of ecclesiastical business. A clericalized laity mistaking "lay responsibility" in the Catholic Church with office-holding in Church bureaucracies is not going to advance the New Evangelization. Neither are clergy who do not grasp that an essential responsibility of the ordained ministers of the Church is to empower the laity for witness and mission.

The next pope will lead the Church beyond clericalism and its deadening effects on mission and evangelization if he patiently but persistently teaches the Catholic world that the basic paradigm of Christian discipleship was established by Mary—and that the many ways of discipleship in the Church all proceed from that Marian profile.

Mary is the first of disciples and the paradigm of
all discipleship because the Marian *fiat*—"Be it done
unto me according to thy word" (Lk 1:38, DV)—
made possible the Incarnation of the Son of God and
thereby defined the character of what it means to
be the Son's disciple: discipleship means conformity
to the divine will for one's life. That pattern was am-
plified and deepened theologically by the last recorded
words of Mary in the New Testament, when, at the
wedding feast in Cana, Mary instructs the wine stewards: "Do whatever he tells you" (Jn 2:5). Pointing
beyond herself and to her son is Mary's role in the
economy of salvation; pointing beyond oneself and
to Mary's son is every disciple's role in the evangelization of the world. At Cana, by pointing to the one
who is both Son of God and son of Mary, Mary points
us into the two central mysteries of Christian faith:
the Incarnation and the Trinity. And in that pointing, Mary—a lay woman without office—established
the pattern for all missionary discipleship, defined the
nature of the Church as a communion of the friends
of the Lord Jesus, and set her son's Gospel at the center of the Church and the Church's work.

Everything else in the Church flows from and is
dependent upon this Marian profile. Pastoral governance as exercised by the successors of the apostle,
and the Petrine office itself, only make Christian sense
in light of the Marian profile of discipleship. The
Pauline model of the Church of evangelization only
makes Christian sense in light of the Marian model of

discipleship. The same is true of the Johannine model of contemplative prayer. A Church that has grasped these New Testament images of the various forms of discipleship and their dependence on the Marian profile of the radically converted disciple will be less likely to get trapped in the kind of internal power struggles that reflect the clericalist distortion of the Christian life, and more likely to get about the work of evangelization.

Clericalism inhibits mission. To lead the Church beyond clericalism, the next pope must lead the Church into a deeper Marian commitment and a more theologically enriched Marian piety.

The next pope will also strengthen the evangelical power of the laity if he encourages a return to the regular practice of the sacramental confession of sins.

The work of evangelization is not easy. Even the most dedicated evangelists fail, and not simply because of hardened hearts but because of their own weakness and sinfulness. Sacramental confession of sins is thus an opportunity for every missionary disciple to lay those failures before the Lord. And in receiving the divine mercy in sacramental absolution, penitents are re-empowered to live out their baptismal responsibility to be witnesses to the Gospel.

Sacramental confession of sins is also an occasion to be reminded of one's baptismal dignity as a Christian. In a Church of sinners, which the Catholic Church emphatically is, guilt can become a great inhibitor of mission. To acknowledge that guilt is not, however, undignified or self-demeaning. To the contrary: all those who go down on their knees to confess their sins and acknowledge their need for grace in order to live out their Christian consecration add to their human dignity by doing so. Thus the next pope must revitalize the Sacrament of Penance in the Church of the twenty-first century, precisely in order to revitalize the laity's sense of mission. He will do so by his own teaching and by encouraging the bishops and priests of the Church to propose the sacramental confession of sins as an essential spiritual discipline: a practice that is ordered to a renewal of one's profession of faith in the Gospel, to a deepening of one's friendship with the Lord Jesus, and thus to a renewal of one's commitment to Christian mission.

In the Church of the New Evangelization, lay Catholics are emphatically not "nonclergy". Lay Catholics are baptized disciples who have been sacramentally invested with Christian dignity, consecrated by the gifts of the Holy Spirit, nourished with grace by the Eucharist, and purified for mission in the Sacrament of Penance. Lay Catholics are friends of the incarnate Son of God and heralds of the Gospel. Lay Catholics are charged with a special responsibility to bring that Gospel to bear in social and cultural life, in public life, and in economic activity. In the Church of the New Evangelization, every Catholic is a missionary disciple who is called to measure the vitality of his or her Christian faith by mission effectiveness.

The next pope must always remind the Catholic faithful that they are, by the Lord's own declaration, the "light of the world" (Mt 5:14). He must also remind the entire Church that, while lay men and women can and should perform many important services within the Church, there is nothing more important for lay Catholics to do than to be heralds of the Gospel and effective witnesses to Jesus Christ in the world—a vocation that will often include marriage and the begetting and evangelizing of children.

A baptized lay Catholic, on whom a great dignity and responsibility has been conferred in the Sacrament of Baptism, is not a second-class Catholic. And that baptismal dignity has an eschatological, or Kingdom, character. For missionary discipleship is the path to the final goal of the Christian life, to which all the baptized are called: the eternal banquet in "the holy city, new Jerusalem" (Rev 21:2), in which the Lamb of God, the Alpha and Omega of the cosmos and history, makes "all things new" (Rev 21:5).

The Next Pope and the
Reform of the Vatican

*When [Jesus] had washed their feet, and taken his
garments, and resumed his place, he said to them,
"Do you know what I have done to you? You call
me Teacher and Lord; and you are right, for so I am.
If I then, your Lord and Teacher, have washed your
feet, you also ought to wash one another's feet. For I
have given you an example, that you also should do
as I have done to you."*

—John 13:12–15

**The next pope must undertake a
thorough administrative and financial
reform of the Holy See.**

Over the past century and a quarter, four popes, beginning with Pope Pius X, have effected (or attempted
to effect) structural reforms in the Church's central
administration, the Roman Curia. Such reforming
efforts must continue. The next pope must see to it
that those structural reforms reflect a proper understanding of the Curia's nature and function.

The Gospel calls everyone in the Church to mission. All Catholics are consecrated for mission by

their baptism. The members of the Church's central administrative staff are no exceptions to this evangelical rule. Each must find his or her way to fulfill the Great Commission.

The Roman Curia is not, however, the place where the evangelical mission of the Church is carried out. The Roman Curia is an instrument of governance whose function is to support the Bishop of Rome in the exercise of his unique Petrine ministry to "strengthen the brethren" (i.e., all the people of the Church) in their lives of service to the Gospel.

This instrument can be designed in any number of ways. That design should not confuse an instrument of governance with a missionary enterprise. As an extension and expression of the *munus regendi* (governing mission) inherent in the Office of Peter, the Roman Curia exists to facilitate the evangelical and missionary work of others throughout the world Church, by facilitating the universal ministry of the Bishop of Rome.

While important for reasons of efficiency, the design of the Roman Curia is of less consequence than the character of the men and women who work in it. Rearranging boxes on an organizational flowchart cannot substitute for appointing officials of sound character to fill those boxes. In the Roman Curia, as everywhere else, personnel *is* policy.

In recent years, financial and sexual scandals have impeded the efficient functioning and damaged the reputation of the Roman Curia. These scandals, which are countersigns to the truths of the Gospel, have done a grave disservice to the Church's evangelical efforts and its capacity to be a moral witness in world affairs. They have also caused considerable distress within the Church, particularly among lay people whose generosity makes possible the work of the various offices in the Vatican.

Thus the next pope must undertake a thorough housecleaning of the Roman Curia. This requires a pope who is a sound judge of character, such that he appoints collaborators of high competence and personal probity after quickly replacing corrupt or malfeasant personnel, whatever their hierarchical rank. The next pope's curial collaborators ought not be chosen on the basis of a clerical or bureaucratic promotion system; no one has a claim to a position of responsibility in the Roman Curia. Rather, the next pope's collaborators should be men and women who have already demonstrated in their local Churches a commitment to the truth of Catholic faith and to honest dealing with others—and who regard work in the Curia as a sacrifice undertaken out of obedience, not as a career path to advancement.

Both of these qualities—doctrinal fidelity and moral rectitude—are crucial to curial reform. For the Roman Curia cannot be an effective instrument of papal governance for the sake of the New Evangelization if its members do not affirm the truths that the Church teaches and live those truths in their own lives.

Clergy and laity who do not believe to be true what the Catholic Church teaches to be true on the basis of revelation and reason have no place in the Church's central administration.

Clergymen and religious men and women who do not faithfully live their vowed commitments to the virtue of chastity and to celibate love have no place in the Roman Curia.

Greedy clergy and laity who see in curial service a means of personal or familial enrichment have no place in the Roman Curia.

No bureaucratic apparatus is perfect, and it would be foolish (or Jansenistic) to expect perfection from the Roman Curia or its members. Nonetheless, the next pope must vigorously address the manifest and manifold curial corruptions that have come to light in recent decades, removing high-ranking (and lower-ranking) officials from their positions if there is evidence of their personal or financial corruption, or both. The next pope must do so for the sake of the Church's evangelical credibility and moral witness. He must also do so for the sake of calling to conversion those whose malfeasance (and worse) in office has wounded their own souls as well as the Church's work.

In undertaking the difficult but essential work of curial reform, the Successor of Peter deserves the support of the entire Church. Thus the next pope has a right to call on his brother bishops for help in finding the best staff possible to aid him in his exercise of the

Office of Peter. His brother bishops have an obligation to answer such queries and, when the answer
involves a priest, the bishop ought to release for service in the Holy See a man whom the pope deems
necessary in fulfilling his Petrine mission.

The next pope would do well to find a principal
collaborator who can help identify the reforms
necessary in the Roman Curia—including the re-
placement of incompetent or corrupt officials—and
then manage the Curia's work so that it becomes an
effective instrument serving the Petrine ministry.

That efficiency will require fostering an atmosphere
of cooperative work that is qualitatively different
from the sense of fear that has sometimes pervaded the
Curia in the past, and from the nepotism and ambi-
tious maneuvering for preference that has too often
characterized aspects of curial life.

There may be structural reforms that mitigate
against dysfunctional tendencies that are a part of
the human condition in any bureaucracy, but which
are especially counterproductive in an organization
whose purpose is to serve the Successor of Peter in
his work of advancing the New Evangelization. Still,
it bears repeating that the critical issue in the effective
functioning of the Roman Curia is the character of
those appointed to work there. The next pope cannot be the personnel manager of the Curia. He must,
however, find a principal collaborator who can do
that essential work for him and with him.

It cannot be overstressed that, in the twenty-first-century world, financial probity at the center of the Church's governance is essential to the Church's proclamation of the Gospel. Great damage has been done to evangelization in the twenty-first century by credible reports of byzantine Vatican financial maneuvers in the international markets and by opaque (or nonexistent) Vatican budgeting and accounting procedures. It is absurd and scandalous that there are vast sums of money in the Holy See that are "off the books", that are invested without proper supervision, and for which there is little or no accountability.

The next pope must end these gross defaults of stewardship, irrespective of the cost to reputations or the short term financial setbacks incurred. What Saint Paul taught the Corinthians two millennia ago remains valid for the Roman Curia today: "This is how one should regard us, as servants of Christ and stewards of the mysteries of God. Moreover it is required of stewards that they be found trustworthy" (1 Cor 4:1–2). Despite the fact that many good and faithful men and women work in the Church's central administration, trust in the financial integrity of the Roman Curia has been badly damaged in recent decades. Repairing the damage, restoring that trust, and taking the drastic action necessary to avoid a full-blown financial crisis in the Holy See must be among the next pope's priorities.

Vatican financial reform is essential in itself. It is also essential for the proclamation of the Gospel. Those

who do not grasp that connection should have nothing to do with the finances of the Holy See.

Restoring trust in the Vatican's financial integrity
will require the next pope to expand the role of financially competent lay men and women in managing
the Holy See's finances. No grade of Holy Orders
confers financial competence. Nor, alas, does Holy
Orders guarantee honest financial dealing. In recent
decades, many advances in reforming the Vatican's
finances have been accomplished by lay people. The
next pope should learn from that.

Curial reform also requires that personnel and
financial resources be redeployed where they are
most needed. To take but one example: In response
to the crimes, sins, and scandals of clerical sexual
abuse, the Congregation for the Doctrine of the Faith
has been given new responsibilities but insufficient
resources to meet those responsibilities. So the Congregation has been overwhelmed by abuse cases and
other cases of clerical misconduct; the work of inves-
tigating and judging those cases proceeds slowly; and
however unfairly, the impression that the Church
continues to lag in addressing clerical sexual abuse
is intensified.

Concurrently, however, new offices have been
added to the Roman Curia, putting a further strain
on human and financial resources.

The next pope should thus mandate a thorough
review of this challenge of matching resources to

responsibilities in the Roman Curia, and he should insist that it be completed within his first six months in the Office of Peter. Lay management expertise will be essential in conducting such a review. Those charged with making recommendations should be assured by the next pope that they must not be afraid to ask a hard but necessary question: "Is this office really necessary for the proper functioning of the Office of Peter in its task of strengthening the brethren for the mission of proclaiming the Gospel?"

Over time, collaborative governance works best, in the Roman Curia as in a local parish, a diocese, or a religious order. It would be well if the next pope had shown a capacity for such collaborative governance in his ministry. At the outset of the next pontificate, however, the pope must clean house in the Roman Curia. Doing this sooner rather than later will be better for all concerned.

The Next Pope, Ecumenism, and Interreligious Dialogue

"I do not pray for these only, but also for those who believe in me through their word, that they may all be one; even as you, Father, are in me, and I in you, that they also may be in us, so that the world may believe that you have sent me. The glory which you have given me I have given to them, that they may be one even as we are one, I in them and you in me, that they may become perfectly one, so that the world may know that you have sent me and have loved them even as you have loved me."

—John 17:20–23

The next pope must strengthen the quest for Christian unity as a quest for unity-in-truth and must facilitate a truth-centered interreligious dialogue.

In the twenty-first-century world to which the Church must proclaim the Gospel and bear witness to the unique salvific role of Jesus Christ, there is considerable confusion about the meaning of "tolerance".

To be tolerant, it is often thought, is to be indifferent to difference, as if differences did not really matter. Fanatical religious movements that murder or discriminate in the name of what they consider sacred reinforce that confusion. If religious wars, religiously motivated violence, or religiously legitimated discrimination are the alternative, many would readily choose the "tolerance" of indifference.

This is not a solution to the challenges posed by the reality of religious difference in the world.

With the exception of the West, the twenty-first-century world is becoming more religious and will likely continue to do so, notwithstanding the misconceptions of Western academics and secularists. To imagine that the solution to the challenges posed by religious difference lies in several billion human beings becoming secular liberals is a fantasy, not a serious prescription for the human future. But even where that fantasy does not dominate the discussion, the false tolerance of indifference not infrequently leads to efforts to ban religious convictions, and the moral understandings that derive from religious convictions, from public life. The result of that (attempted) ban is often more intolerance, more misunderstanding, and more violence, when it does not lead to a soft (or even hard) form of totalitarianism.

Etymology offers a clue to a better understanding of the challenge of religious difference.

The root of the English word "tolerance" is the Latin verb *tolerare*, which means to "bear with" or "suffer with". That root sheds light on true tolerance. It suggests that tolerance, rightly understood, is not indifference to difference, which often demeans the beliefs of the "other" and thereby makes conflict more likely or more intense. Rather, true tolerance is engaging the "other" within a bond of civility, in a mutual search for the truth of things, including the religious truth of things. This is admittedly a difficult lesson to learn, but the world must learn it. The Catholic Church can support that learning by teaching the true meaning of tolerance and embodying it in its ecumenical and interreligious relations.

The next pope must grasp the nature of true tolerance. In his exchange with those who are religiously "other", he must manifest a civility that aims at a mutual clarification of truth, even as he holds firm to the truths that it has been given him to safeguard. However difficult, this is the ecumenical and interreligious witness the next pope must give. For unless he leads ecumenical and interreligious dialogues that take these exercises beyond exchanges of mutual regard to robust, civil explorations of the truth, his ecumenical and interreligious efforts will do little to advance the cause of genuine tolerance.

In the field of Christian ecumenism, the next pope should consider whether the fruits of the old ecumenical dialogues with mainline or liberal Protestantism have been harvested.

These dialogues have not brought about the unity of the Church for which Christ prayed, and which was one of Pope John XXIII's goals in summoning the

Second Vatican Council. Over the past half-century, bilateral Catholic/mainline Protestant ecumenical dialogues have clarified important theological issues, defused misunderstandings, and led to far more cordial relations between Catholicism and many Reformation communities. These are important achievements. Welcome as they are, however, those achievements have not significantly advanced the cause of full, visible Christian unity.

For that unity can only be built upon truth, and it has proven impossible to achieve unity-in-truth with mainline or liberal Protestant denominations whose understanding of Christian truth is constantly changing. This shifting of doctrinal and moral boundaries within liberal Protestant communities seems likely to continue over the course of the twenty-first century. Thus the next pope should consider a redeployment of Catholicism's ecumenical energies within the Western Christian communities toward a more intense ecumenical engagement with the growing parts of world Protestantism: the evangelical, Pentecostal, and fundamentalist Protestant communities.

Such a redeployment, leading to serious theological dialogue, will take considerable time. Old shibboleths and myths about Catholic belief and practice that have largely disappeared from mainline Protestant denominations remain more or less intact in evangelical, Pentecostalist, and fundamentalist Protestant communities. Nor are these communities organized in such a way as to support ongoing theological conversations of the sort to which the Catholic Church has become accustomed with mainline denominations. Still, informal and unofficial efforts in North America and elsewhere have demonstrated that serious theological exchange can be created between Catholics and evangelical, Pentecostal, and fundamentalist Protestants. The next pope should become aware of those efforts, if he is not already. And he should consider whether ecumenical conversations conducted outside the normal ecclesiastical bureaucracies are the path forward in this field, at least for the foreseeable future.

The next pope should also consider a reconfiguration of the Catholic Church's dialogue with Orthodox Christianity.

While there are cordial relations between the Holy See in Rome and the Ecumenical Patriarchate of Constantinople—a respect and affection embodied in the exchange of high-ranking delegations every year on the patronal feasts of Saints Peter and Paul (in Rome) and Saint Andrew (in Istanbul)—the Vatican has often put heavier emphasis in East-West ecumenism on the Catholic dialogue with Russian Orthodoxy. The assumption seems to have been that, as the Moscow Patriarchate leads the numerically largest of the Orthodox Churches, it should be the principal Orthodox ecumenical interlocutor with the Church of Rome, de facto if not de iure.

This next pope must reexamine this assumption, which has led to unnecessary difficulties and even betrayals. The Patriarchate of Moscow remains firmly under the control of the Russian state, and its principal ecumenical officer is not infrequently a spokesman for twenty-first-century Kremlin imperialism, giving it a religious or cultural gloss. Thus the Rome-Moscow dialogue is structurally imbalanced, even false, in that Catholic churchmen who wield no worldly power are in conversation with Russian Orthodox churchmen who (irrespective of their personal religious convictions) function as agents of Russian state power.

Vatican coddling of Russian myths and pretensions has also led to the Holy See being less than stalwart in its support of the Eastern Catholic Churches in full communion with the Bishop of Rome. This Roman reticence has especially impacted the largest of the Eastern Catholic Churches, the Ukrainian Greek Catholic Church, which the Russian Orthodox Church (in league with the Soviet security service) tried to liquidate in 1946. Pusillanimity in the face of Russian Orthodox aggressiveness is unworthy of the Holy See. The next pope should put a stop to it, insisting politely but firmly on an ecumenical dialogue with Russian Orthodoxy that is truth-centered theologically and truth-based historically.

Such a re-framed dialogue would also be useful in fostering those currents of thought within world Orthodoxy that seek a path beyond Orthodoxy's traditional deference to, if not entire dependence upon, state power. Orthodox thinkers in Russia and Ukraine have shown an interest in Catholic social doctrine and the Catholic church-state theory that has evolved since Vatican II's Declaration on Religious Freedom. The next pope should encourage deeper and more frequent ecumenical conversations with those creative and courageous Orthodox thinkers.

Interreligious dialogue in a season of heightened and politicized religiosity is complex, volatile, and sometimes dangerous. The next pope will best advance what is possible in interreligious dialogue if he declines to add the burden of false images and tropes to already difficult conversations.

Thus the next pope should consider laying to rest, within the Holy See and in its work, the false trope that there are "three Abrahamic religions": an image that suggests a triad in which each of the three parts thinks of the others in the same way. That is simply not true. Catholicism's relationship with Judaism is qualitatively different than its relationship with Islam; that qualitative difference is a matter of divine revelation, not human opinion or historical accident. Islam, for its part, is far more supersessionist toward both Christianity and Judaism than orthodox Christian theology ever was about Judaism. Thus the "three Abrahamic faiths" trope obscures far more than it illuminates.

To be sure, when viewed from the perspective of a Buddhist, a Hindu, a Confucian, or a follower of Shinto, Judaism, Christianity, and Islam manifest certain family resemblances that may make them seem cousins of a sort. But the Bishop of Rome (who is not a Buddhist, a Hindu, a Confucian, or a follower of Shinto) should not reinforce by his words or actions the false idea that Judaism, Christianity, and Islam are three branches on a single monotheistic tree. That is not how each of these monotheistic faiths has understood itself historically, and the reasons why run to each faith's understanding of divine revelation. Thus a truth-centered dialogue among the three, or between any two parts of the alleged triad, is impeded, not fostered, by the notion that there are "three Abrahamic faiths" whose differences are matters of accent or ethnicity or historical contingency.

Genuine interreligious dialogue begins with understanding and acknowledging the "other's" self-understanding; it is not advanced by false tropes. The next pope should move Catholicism beyond the "three Abrahamic faiths" imagery, precisely for the sake of a truth-centered interreligious encounter. The notion of a monotheistic triad has no deep roots in the theology of any of the three faiths; it was created in the twentieth century by academics; and the next pope should see to it that it does not frame Catholicism's dialogue with Islam in the twenty-first century.

The Next Pope and World Affairs

For God sent the Son into the world, not to condemn the world, but that the world might be saved through him.

—John 3:17

The next pope must grasp the basic dynamics of twenty-first-century world politics and the global economy, and must recognize that the Church's only leverage in world affairs is moral leverage.

There are many providential ironies in the past two hundred years of Catholic history. Prominent among them is the irony that political modernity, various expressions of which tried to erase the Catholic Church from the pages of history, liberated Catholicism for bolder evangelical mission and more effective public witness in public life by ending the Church's Babylonian captivity to state power.

The key moment in this providential irony, which has profoundly shaped the modern exercise of the Office of Peter, was the demise of the Papal States in 1870. What seemed catastrophic to some Catholics then—and what looked to some of the *bien-pensants* of that era like the end of Catholicism's role in shaping history—in fact freed the papacy to play the role of moral teacher and moral witness in world affairs: a far more consequential role than popes had played in the early modern period as absolute monarchs of a grade-D European power. That reformed role was most dramatically exercised by Pope John Paul II, who helped shape the nonviolent revolution that brought an end to European communism. But the role of global moral authority and teacher has been exercised, with varying degrees of success, by every pope since Leo XIII.

The next pope must understand this history and the lessons it teaches.

Among the most important developments of modern Catholic history has been the evolution of the Church's capacity to order its own internal life by the free appointment of bishops, without the interference of state powers.

In the middle of the nineteenth century, Pope Pius IX had an unencumbered right of episcopal appointment in the city of Rome and four countries, three of which were Protestant. Deft Vatican diplomacy over the next century and a half led to a much better situation, and in the early twenty-first century the pope has a free right of appointment virtually everywhere (the exceptions being Vietnam and China). That right of appointment is sometimes complicated in Europe by long-standing concordats or the ancient prerogatives of local Churches. In the main, however, the Catholic Church throughout the world has regained the authority to order its own life by it own criteria.

For the sake of the Gospel and the Church's evangelical mission, this is an achievement and a freedom that the next pope must zealously protect. In doing so, he will be conducting the Office of Peter according to the mind of the Second Vatican Council and the prescriptions of the 1983 Code of Canon Law. In *Christus Dominus* (Christ the Lord), Vatican II's Decree on the Pastoral Office of Bishops in the Church, the Council Fathers determined that "in order to safeguard the liberty of the Church and to better and more effectively promote the good of the faithful ... no rights or privileges [are to] be conceded to the civil authorities, in regard to the election, nomination, or presentation of bishops."[1] This teaching was then codified in Canon 377.5 of the Code of Canon Law.

The purpose of this conciliar teaching and this law is the protection of the Church's evangelical mission. State-authorized bishops, especially in totalitarian societies, lack full freedom to proclaim the Gospel. In circumstances where Catholics have heroically resisted state attempts to control the Church by controlling the appointment of its ordained leaders, Vatican diplomacy undercuts the Church's evangelical message and mission when it ignores the teaching of Vatican II and the Church's own law for the sake of accommodating the demands of authoritarian or totalitarian regimes.

Thus the next pope must insist on the Church's final authority in the appointment of bishops, anywhere and everywhere. In rare circumstances, the appointment process may involve prudential consultation with state authorities. But that consultation cannot mean that the state or a political party has the first right of nomination, to which the Church then responds. For the sake of the Gospel, that sort of arrangement cannot be countenanced. Where it is, the next pope should end the practice, reaffirming the Catholic Church's commitment to the teaching of *Christus Dominus* and the prohibitions contained in the Code of Canon Law.

The next pope must also undertake a reconsideration of the theory and practice of Vatican diplomacy.

The diplomatic service of the Holy See—the Vatican nuncios, apostolic delegates, and other papal representatives to governments or international organizations—perform many useful functions. In countries where an embattled local Church is under political pressure, papal diplomats can be a lifeline to Rome and the global audience the pope commands. In international organizations, Vatican diplomacy can usefully remind those who wield power that the exercise of power always has a moral component. The contemporary world ought to have learned some bitter lessons from the detachment of power from moral principle; Vatican diplomatic representation (and papal addresses to international organizations) can help draw those lessons and point out their relevance to the burning issues of the moment.

That will only happen, however, when the pope and the Church's diplomats recognize that the only leverage the papacy and the Holy See have in world affairs is moral leverage.

This truth has not been sufficiently understood in Vatican diplomatic circles. Papal diplomats (especially Italian papal diplomats) often think and act as if they were still representing the Papal States, a minor European power, rather than the Holy See, the juridical embodiment of the universal pastoral ministry of the Bishop of Rome. This confusion has led to making unnecessary and sometimes scandalous concessions to authoritarian or totalitarian governments, under the misconception that such concessions keep Vatican diplomacy "in play". In fact, all those concessions do is underscore diplomatic weakness and a lack of evangelical and moral resolve.

It is striking, for example, that rising Vatican diplomats are taught that the Vatican's *Ostpolitik* toward European communism in the 1970s—a strategy of gradual concessions to communist governments—was a great success that paved the way for the nonviolent Revolution of 1989 in Central and Eastern Europe. That is simply false. The *Ostpolitik* had no measurable success in the countries of the Warsaw Pact. To the contrary, it led to the demoralization of the Church in several countries, the control of local hierarchies

by communist parties, and the deep penetration of
the Vatican by Warsaw Pact secret intelligence services. Such a gross misunderstanding of modern Vatican diplomatic history is not without contemporary
consequences, for it has underwritten concessions that
never should have been made to twenty-first-century
totalitarian regimes.

Thus the next pope should commission a thorough review of the successes and failures of Holy
See diplomacy since World War II, drawing on the
expertise of lay historians as well as churchmen.

Such a review would also do well to consider the
theory and practice of Vatican diplomacy in international organizations, where the present pattern
involves the Holy See taking a position on virtually
everything. Given that the only leverage the Church
brings to bear in those circumstances is moral leverage, prioritizing the Holy See's concerns at the United
Nations and similar venues might well be a wiser
course. For if the Holy See takes a position on virtually every issue, that tends to suggest that all issues are
equal, which, from the point of view of moral reason-
ing, is certainly not true. It also tends to suggest that
the Catholic Church has relevant expertise on virtually
every issue of international public policy, which is also
not true.

The next pope should also give careful thought to
his own diplomatic interventions. Absolutist papal
positions can have the unintended effect of shrinking

the available political space for reasonable policies that make incremental progress. There are, obviously, issues on which a firm and uncompromising papal stance is not only desirable but imperative: the inalienable right to life from conception until natural death; the defense of religious freedom for all; the imperative of ending human trafficking. Not all issues are so clear, however. Vatican diplomacy and papal actions on the world stage should recognize that.

Both papal interventions and Vatican diplomacy will be more effective in the twenty-first century if the next pope and those who represent him speak from a well-sourced fund of knowledge about contemporary political and economic realities.

It is imperative, for example, that the next pope and the Church he leads be vigorous in their defense of the poor. That defense will be more readily heard if it is accompanied by an acknowledgment that much of the world has become not-poor in the past fifty years, and if it is based on a recognition that the reason for this is that more and more people have been incorporated into the networks where wealth is created and exchanged. Such an acknowledgment and recognition is not a concession to one or another economic theory or ideology; that people become not-poor when they are empowered to participate in the world's networks of production and exchange is taught by the social doctrine of the Church.

The world of the twenty-first century badly needs the Church's voice in defense of the dignity of the human person and the implications of that dignity for the proper ordering of political and economic life. The next pope should see to it that the Church's voice, whether it is his voice or the Holy See's, is a fully informed voice. Here, too, is an arena of Catholic witness in which the next pope would do well to draw on lay expertise—the expertise of those who are fully committed to the Church's moral teaching and social ethic and who are professionally knowledgeable about politics and economics.

Centered on Christ and the Gospel

*He is the image of the invisible God, the first-born
of all creation; for in him all things were created, in
heaven and on earth, visible and invisible, whether
thrones or dominions or principalities or authorities—
all things were created through him and for him.
He is before all things, and in him all things hold
together. He is the head of the body, the Church; he
is the beginning, the first-born from the dead, that in
everything he might be pre-eminent. For in him all
the fulness of God was pleased to dwell, and through
him to reconcile to himself all things, whether on earth
or in heaven, making peace by the blood of his cross.*

—Colossians 1:15–20

The world typically sees the Catholic Church as a
vast, complex global organization. More than a few
Catholics also think of the Church that way. The
entirety of modern Catholic history, however, has
been pointing the Church in another direction and
asking the Church to think of itself in a different way.

In a Spirit-led and Spirit-guided movement of evangelical renewal, the Catholic Church has been and is
being called to be radically Christocentric and evangelical. The Church is being summoned to put every

facet of its organized life at the service of the Gospel, the proclamation of the Kingdom of God among us, and the offer of friendship with the Lord Jesus Christ, who is the reason for the Church's existence.

All authentic Catholic reform is a return to the Church's originating "form", given it by Christ himself. At the center of that "form" is the Great Commission to go and make disciples of all nations. The recovery of this foundational truth about the Church is the bright thread connecting the past 150 years of Catholic history, from Pope Leo XIII through the Second Vatican Council and into the twenty-first century. The Christ-centeredness of the Church, which implies the evangelical imperative, is also the bright thread connecting these reflections on the Office of Peter and its exercise in a Church in mission.

The Petrine Office is unlike any other position of great responsibility in the world. That office is the source of all executive, legislative, and judicial authority in the Catholic Church. Yet the man who sits in the Chair of Peter is not the master of the Catholic tradition but its servant. He must lead from within that tradition and nurture its development. But he must not imagine that he is above the tradition or the Gospel, for then he and the Church are in grave peril.

And then there is the range of his responsibility. As the title "supreme *pontiff*" suggests, the pope must somehow be a bridge between God and humanity, between the Catholic Church and other religious communities, between the Catholic Church and civil governments, between his own office and the bishops with whom he forms a governing college in the Church, and between the center of the Church's administration and 1.1 billion Catholics living in virtually every imaginable circumstance on this planet.

And he must eventually give an account of his leadership and his stewardship, not to an electorate, but to the living God.

The task may seem impossible. In human terms, it is. That is why the next pope, like those of his predecessors who have best answered the Lord's call to Peter to "strengthen your brethren", must be a man transparent to the grace of God in his life, for only that grace will enable him to teach, sanctify, and govern as the Successor of Peter should.

The fourth-century Father of the Church Saint Gregory of Nyssa saw this clearly, as the Church reminds itself every year in the Liturgy of the Hours:

> We shall be blessed with clear vision if we keep our eyes fixed on Christ, for he, as Paul teaches, is our head, and there is in him no shadow of evil. Saint Paul himself and all who have reached the same heights of sanctity had their eyes fixed on Christ, and so have all who live and move and have their being in him.
>
> As no darkness can be seen by anyone surrounded by light, so no trivialities can capture the attention of anyone who has his eyes on Christ. The man

who keeps his eyes upon the head and origin of the whole universe has them on virtue in all its perfection; he has them on truth, on justice, on immortality and on everything else that is good, for Christ is goodness itself.[1]

Thus the next pope must be, above all, a radically converted disciple: a man formed in the depth of his being by the conviction that Jesus Christ is the incarnate Son of God, who reveals to the world the face of God the merciful Father and the truth about humanity, its dignity, and its destiny. The intensity of the next pope's relationship with the Lord Jesus, and the wisdom of his discernment of what the Lord Jesus is asking of him at any given moment, will determine whether his papacy advances the cause of the Gospel or frustrates the Church's evangelical mission.

That is why the next pope needs, and deserves, the prayerful support of the entire Catholic world.

"Go therefore and make disciples of all nations, baptizing them in the name of the Father and of the Son and of the Holy Spirit."

—Matthew 28:19

And they went forth and preached everywhere, while the Lord worked with them and confirmed the message by the signs that attended it. Amen.

—Mark 16:20

ENDNOTES

The Holy Spirit and This Catholic Moment

1. John XXIII, address *Gaudet Mater Ecclesia* (Mother Church Rejoices) (October 11, 1962), no. 8.

2. Ibid., no. 3.

3. Ibid., no. 15.

4. Ibid.

5. Ibid., no. 17.

6. See Lucas Moreira Cardinal Neves, O.P., "Evangelii Nuntiandi: Paul VI's Pastoral Testament to the Church", EWTN .com, taken from *L'Osservatore Romano*, Weekly Edition in English, January 17, 2001, p. 10, https://www.ewtn.com/cathol icism/library/evangelii-nuntiandi-paul-vis-pastoral-testament -to-the-church-1983. The article is a reflection on the twenty-fifth anniversary of the publication of *Evangelii Nuntiandi*.

7. Paul VI, apostolic exhortation *Evangelii Nuntiandi* (Announcing the Gospel) (December 8, 1975), no. 22.

8. "The Final Report of the 1985 Extraordinary Synod; The Church, in the Word of God, Celebrates the Mysteries of Christ for the Salvation of the World", EWTN.com, accessed March 17, 2020, https://www.ewtn.com/catholicism/library /final-report-of-the-1985-extraodinary-synod-2561.

9. Ibid.

10. John Paul II, apostolic letter *Novo Millennio Ineunte* (Entering the New Millennium) (January 6, 2001), no. 1.

The Next Pope and the New Evangelization

1. Vatican Council II, Dogmatic Constitution on the Church, *Lumen Gentium* (The Light of the Nations) (November 21, 1964), no. 2.

2. Ibid., no. 6.

3. Ibid.

4. Ibid.

5. Ibid.

6. Ibid.

7. Ibid., no. 3.

8. Vatican Council II, Constitution on the Sacred Liturgy, *Sacrosanctum Concilium* (The Constitution on the Sacred Liturgy) (December 4, 1963), no. 2.

9. John Paul II, encyclical letter *Fides et Ratio* (Faith and Reason) (September 14, 1998), opening sentence.

10. Vatican Council II, Dogmatic Constitution on Divine Revelation, *Dei Verbum* (The Word of God) (November 18, 1965), chap. 2, nos. 7, 9–10.

11. *Lumen Gentium*, no. 3.

The Next Pope and the Office of Peter

1. Homily of His Holiness John Paul II for the Inauguration of His Pontificate (October 22, 1978), no. 2, http://www.vatican.va/content/john-paul-ii/en/homilies/1978/documents/hf_jp-ii_hom_19781022_inizio-pontificato.html.

2. Ibid., no. 4.

3. Ibid.

4. Ibid., no. 5.

5. Cited in Patrick Granfield, *The Limits of the Papacy: Authority and Autonomy in the Church* (New York: Crossroad, 1987), pp. 62–63.

6. Ibid.

The Next Pope, the Crisis of the Human Person, and Christian Humanism

1. Henri de Lubac, *The Drama of Atheist Humanism* (San Francisco: Ignatius Press, 1995), p. 15.

2. Christopher Dawson, "The Modern Dilemma", in *Christianity and European Culture: Selections from the Work of Christopher Dawson*, ed. Gerald Russello (Washington, D.C.: Catholic University of America Press, 1988), p. 118.

3. Vatican Council II, Pastoral Constitution on the Church in the Modern World, *Gaudium et Spes* (Joy and Hope) (December 7, 1965), no. 22.

4. Ibid., no. 24.

The Next Pope and the Bishops

1. *Lumen Gentium*, nos. 20, 24–25.

2. John Paul II, encyclical *Evangelium Vitae* (The Gospel of Life) (March 25, 1995).

The Next Pope and the Church's Priests

1. *Lumen Gentium*, no. 11.

2. *Sacrosanctum Concilium*, no. 8.

The Next Pope and World Affairs

1. Vatican Council II, Decree on the Pastoral Office of Bishops in the Church, *Christus Dominus* (Christ the Lord) (October 28, 1965), no. 20.

Centered on Christ and the Gospel

1. From a Homily on Ecclesiastes by Saint Gregory of Nyssa, Bishop (Hom. 5:PG 44, 683–86), Office of Readings, Monday of the Seventh Week in Ordinary Time, in *The Liturgy of the Hours*, copyright © 1973, 1974, 1975 by International Commission on English in the Liturgy Corporation.